Facing
Loneliness

Discovery House

P U B L I S H E R S

BOX 3566 • GRAND RAPIDS, MI 49501

*PUBLISHING BOOKS THAT FEED
THE SOUL WITH THE WORD OF GOD.*

Facing Loneliness

The Starting Point of a New Journey

by
J. Oswald Sanders

Facing Loneliness
Copyright © 1988 by Highland Books

Discovery House edition published in 1990 by agreement with
Highland Books, Crowborough, East Sussex, England.

Discovery House publishers is affiliated with Radio Bible Class,
Grand Rapids, Michigan.

Discovery House books are distributed to the trade by
Thomas Nelson Publishers, Nashville, Tennessee 37214.

Library of Congress Cataloging-in-Publication Data

Sanders, J. Oswald (John Oswald), 1902—
    Facing Loneliness: the starting point of a new journey/
by J. Oswald Sanders

        p.   cm.

    ISBN: 0-913367-37-0
    1. Loneliness—Religious aspects—Christianity. I. Title.
    BV4911.S263   1990
    248.8'6—dc20
                                                        89-48234
                                                              CIP

Unless otherwise indicated, all Scripture quotations are from the
New International Version. Copyright © 1973, 1978, 1984 by the
International Bible Society. Used by permission of Zondervan Bible
Publishers.

Printed in the United States of America

CONTENTS

PREFACE

Loneliness is not a pleasant subject to write about. Nor is it a pleasant emotion to experience.

When I was asked to write on this subject, although the experience of twice losing a loved wife and seventeen years spent as a widower had afforded personal experience of its poignancy, I shrank from the task. Others have done it, and doubtless done it better. But mounting experience with so many lonely souls in different lands and in different walks of life has impressed me deeply with the enormity and universality of the problem. And too few seem to have discovered a satisfying solution. So, reluctantly, I have taken up my pen, in the hope that something I write may help to calm the pangs of loneliness for some readers.

I know there is no simple or single answer to the problem, no glib solution; for while the root cause is the same, the contributory factors are many. It is a complex phenomenon, and different types of loneliness require different approaches. Relief will be found only when we go beyond symptoms and deal with the toxic center from which the malady springs. The lack of intimacy, which is one of the most painful elements, must be addressed and remedied.

Ultimately, loneliness stems from mankind's alienation from God, so no remedy that does not take this factor into account will afford more than superficial and temporary relief. But while the condition is rooted in the spiritual, the relevant psychological and social elements must not be overlooked.

The first part of the book is devoted mainly to an endeavor to isolate the causes of the malady, and the second to suggesting avenues of help for the individual needs of people. However, I have not confined the helpful suggestions to the second part.

The resources available to lonely people, both from God and from fellow men and women, are more abundant than they realize and would discover if they made the attempt. Did they but realize it, their loneliness could be the starting point of a new journey toward moral and spiritual maturity. If they would abandon the search for someone to care for them, and set themselves instead to care for someone else, they would be amazed to discover that their loneliness was quite bearable, even if it was not entirely banished.

PART 1:
ISOLATING THE CAUSES

1

DIAGNOSING THE MALADY

Once a philosophical problem contemplated by
poets and prophets, loneliness is now a universal
condition for millions of Americans. Not only for
the elderly and divorced, but also for the men
and women filled with the ache of loneliness
within their marriages. It is fast becoming an
American tradition.
—Tim Timmons, *Loneliness Is Not a Disease*

Diagnosis precedes prescription. It is only when the
physician has made a correct diagnosis that he will
be in a position to prescribe the appropriate remedy.
It is no different with maladies of the spirit. Accord-
ingly, the first section of this book aims at uncover-
ing some of the causes of the universal malady of
loneliness.

Loneliness is more readily experienced than
defined. The Webster's Dictionary definition is:
"Being without company; cut off from others; not fre-
quented by human beings; sad from being alone;
producing a feeling of bleakness or desolation."
Taken together, these concepts combine to describe a
dismal yet painfully common experience. It is not
without reason that *loneliness* has been termed the

most desolate word in the English language. Its very sound seems to echo its own desolation.

One of its distressing features is that its victims are usually unable to diagnose the nature and source of their malady, and as a consequence are unable to discover an appropriate remedy. However, this should not discourage us from endeavoring to trace its tortuous course and hopefully discover ways in which its harmful effects can be subdued, or even totally eliminated.

Loneliness assumes many forms, each equally undesirable—an unsatisfied inner ache, an inner vacuum, a craving for satisfaction. The human heart has an insatiable longing to be loved.

Research has revealed that the experiences most conducive to acute loneliness are: the death of a life partner or other family member; a separation or divorce; a broken engagement; leaving one's homeland for a new country. All of these incur deep emotional trauma.

In other cases the loneliness unconsciously reflects a person's inability to initiate or maintain a stable and satisfying relationship, especially with members of the opposite sex. But whatever the cause, the experience is painful in the extreme.

At one of his crusades, the Latin American evangelist Luis Palau asked the people in his audience to indicate the subject on which they would most like him to speak. A number of themes were suggested, but the majority requested him to speak on the subject of loneliness.

They were giving voice to the plight of many who suffer from one of the most pervasive and emotional disorders of our times. Its growing prevalence in the last half-century warrants careful investigation of both cause and possible cure. Of course loneliness has always plagued mankind, but the special conditions that prevail in our times have increased its incidence enormously.

One of the frequent side effects is a sense of emptiness and futility that nothing seems to dispel. Contemporary social and environmental factors are often the villain of the piece. For older people the breaking up of the family home, with the consequent loss of familiar friends and scenes, can prove a traumatic experience. They feel rootless and find it desperately difficult to strike up a new relationship in strange surroundings.

In her article for *Mental Hygiene* titled "Loneliness in Old Age," Irene Burnside contends that "loneliness is the state of mind in which the fact that there were people in one's life in the past is more or less forgotten, and the hope that there may be interpersonal relations in the future is out of the realm of expectation."

It is no sin to be lonely, so there is no need to add a sense of guilt to the problem. Our sinless Lord was lonely. But if the facts of the case are not faced realistically and purposefully, harmful attitudes may develop that will hinder present enjoyment of life and fruitful service for God and man in the future.

THE SEEDS OF LONELINESS

It is rather surprising to discover that despite its universality in past ages as well as in our own, loneliness is nowhere treated at length in the Bible. Illustrations of its ravages, however, abound. The Scriptures alone provide us with a credible and authentic diagnosis of mankind's fundamental problems, so it must be to the Bible that we look for both diagnosis and cure.

The biblical record asserts that in his original state, Adam was perfect in form and intelligence.

> So God created man in his own image, in the image of God he created him; male and female he created them. . . . God saw all that he had made and it was very good (Gen. 1:27, 31).

But though he came perfect from the hand of God, Adam was still finite and incomplete. This is implicit in the first recorded statement from the mouth of God.

> The Lord God said, *"It is not good for the man to be alone.* I will make a helper suitable for him."* . . . So the Lord God caused the man to fall into a deep sleep; and while he was sleeping, he took one of the man's ribs and closed up the place with flesh. Then the Lord God made a woman from the rib he had taken out of the man, and he brought her to the man" (Gen. 2:18, 21–22; *italics mine*).

In their original innocence, Adam and Eve lived without shame or fear. They enjoyed uninhibited companionship with each other and with the Lord God. They were neither alone nor lonely.

Into this ideal scene the serpent subtly introduced himself and successfully seduced them into sin. This, in turn, resulted in the forfeiture of their perfection and innocence, for it was an act of rebellion against their Creator and Benefactor. Henceforth they were fallen beings, and involved the whole human race in their fall. But though the image of God in them was sadly defaced, it was not totally obliterated. In that pregnant moment loneliness was born.

The immediate result of their sin and folly was banishment from the Garden of Eden. From then on they were enmeshed in the tentacles of fear and gripped by the icy fingers of loneliness. Tragic exchange! Desolating loneliness for intimacy with God!

MANKIND'S TWOFOLD NEED

People were created with a twofold need—fellowship with God and companionship with other human beings. For these, if they are to realize the full purpose of His creation, there can be no substitute. The social instinct is deep within every human being and when this need remains unsatisfied, the seeds of loneliness grow and flourish.

We are vulnerable to the onslaught of loneliness on a number of levels, of which the emotional is the most distressing because it involves the loss of close relationship with other people. It can be relieved only by establishing some alternative, congenial association. To those who are by nature shy or reserved, this presents an almost insurmountable obstacle.

Social loneliness is related to the contacts we have—or do not have—with the community in which we live. This is a chronic sense of being "left out," and this in turn generates a feeling of low self-worth. The victim labors under the conviction—by no means always justified—that he or she is of little significance to anyone, and therefore no one desires his or her friendship. This attitude often leads to a largely self-imposed isolation.

What people in this state of mind most need is a group of caring and supportive friends; but how and where can they find them? In many churches this need is met in home groups, whose members exercise a mutual interest in the others' welfare. But the initial step—the joining of such a group—is the decision of the sufferer.

Though social loneliness is undoubtedly distressing, spiritual loneliness is even more fundamental to the condition, for it carries with it the feeling of isolation not only from fellow men and women but from the God who alone can fill the vacuum in the human heart.

Blaise Pascal, the noted French scientist, held that in every human heart there exists a God-shaped vacuum. Centuries before him, Augustine, Bishop of Hippo, put his finger on the root cause of loneliness: "God created man for Himself and our hearts are restless until they find rest in Him."

For this reason, the greatest need of the lonely person is to ensure that he or she is in a right relationship with God, the Great Physician. He has a cure for every lack and malady of the human heart, whether it be spiritual or social.

CONTRIBUTORY CAUSES

In our indulgent and affluent western society, where most can gratify their every desire, it seems unexplainable that so many are victims of the scourge of loneliness and that it is as prevalent among the rich as among the poor. Many factors have combined to produce this effect.

Sweeping changes in the social structure of society have contributed their quota. Unprecedented mobility on land and in the air has encouraged this trend. Every year, twenty percent of a community living in an urban situation change their location. This inevitably precipitates the break-up of family groups and hinders the development of a community spirit and the forming of enduring friendships.

Modern technology and the magic of the microchip have added immeasurably to the complexity and yet uniformity of modern life. Everything tends to grow more impersonal. The old corner store, with its personal attention and service, has given way to the relentless competition of the supermarket. The mass production line has reduced many skillful workers to the status of human robots. The competent tradesman, who used to take pride in his work, has been made redundant, or forced into early retirement. Following is how one unwilling retiree expressed his feelings:

> Since I have retired from life's competition
> Each day is filled with complete repetition,

I get up each morning and dust off my wits,
Go, pick up the paper and read the obits.
If my name isn't there, I know I'm not dead.
I get a good breakfast and go back to bed.

Paradoxically, the rapid urbanization of the world—a modern phenomenon that has spawned 300 cities of more than one million citizens—while forcing people to live closer together physically, has resulted in even greater social isolation. According to the census taken in 1982, only about twenty percent of the people in China lived in city centers. By 1986 the proportion shot up to thirty-seven percent.

The stark high-rise apartment blocks of the mega-cities are characterized more by fear and suspicion than by friendship and neighborliness. There are, of course, glorious exceptions to this generalization, but it is, sadly, very near the truth. Is it not a strange anomaly that large numbers of people can live shoulder to shoulder, and yet at the same time be gripped by intense loneliness? Yet such is the case.

THE TELEVISION INVASION

Television has proved a mixed blessing. Like many other inventions that have great potential for good, television has been exploited—one could say prostituted—by greedy and unprincipled people for selfish and often evil purposes. One of its destructive effects is that habitual viewers seldom communicate with one another in a meaningful way. Superficial viewing habits are formed that inhibit intelligent conversation and deep thought.

A great many of the programs presented are not merely senseless, but positively harmful. Violence and pornography slip through the censor's net and intrude uninvited into the homes of the people. As a direct consequence we are reaping the harvest in a sharply rising rate of crime.

Altogether apart from these crudely adverse features, viewers are encouraged to live in a world of fantasy. Instead of enjoying genial and congenial action and interaction with family and friends, many live their lives vicariously in the lives of the television actors and actresses, be they good or bad. When parents who are concerned about the intellectual and moral standards presented to their children attempt to monitor the programs, the result is very often family discord.

These factors involved in the television invasion combine to provide a fertile culture bed for loneliness.

LONELINESS IS UNIVERSAL

"It is strange to be known so universally, and yet to be so lonely." These poignant words were spoken by the great scientist Albert Einstein and demonstrate that loneliness invades the lives of the great and intellectual as well as those in lower stations of life. It is no respecter of persons. But perhaps it was Einstein's very brilliance that isolated him from lesser mortals and gave birth to his loneliness.

Perhaps more than at any time in history, this scourge has become pervasive in the world and not less among the sophisticated than among primitive societies. It is a rapidly increasing part of human existence, an inescapable fact of life. Loneliness seems to keep pace with social and industrial change in today's world. It has been accurately described as a debilitating deficiency disease that knows no limitations of age, class, or sex.

In an effort to discover the type of problem that was of most concern to its readers, an American newspaper conducted a broad survey. In the responses received, three problems predominated. They were—in order of priority—fear, worry, loneliness. In the last of the three there are elements of the first two as well. But it is loneliness that casts the longest shadow on our contemporary world.

In a poll conducted among patients in a psychiatric hospital, almost eighty percent claimed that it was loneliness that drove them to seek help from the psychiatrist. It is small wonder that in his book *Overcoming Loneliness*, David Jeremiah termed it "the disease of the decade, perhaps of every decade in our mid and late twentieth century."

A large number of modern pop songs and lyrics are shot through with the melancholy themes of frustration, emptiness, loneliness. Much of the accompanying music is set in the minor key and is a reflection of the negative aspects of life. Country and western music majors in broken relationships, desertion, and infidelity. All this tells its own story.

THE RACIAL MIX
The impact of the electronic age, the widening reach of the media and communications, and the burgeoning population in many nations have thrown people together to a degree never before experienced. The

racial mix in many mega-cities is almost unbeliev-able. I was speaking recently with the principal of a high school in Los Angeles who said that among his student body no fewer than fifty-two ethnic groups were represented!

Instead of eliminating loneliness, as one would expect, this inescapable contact of the races has served only to exacerbate it. There seems to be little desire in most ethnic groups to overleap racial and cultural barriers. Too often it is a case of physical proximity without emotional intimacy.

Foreign students in western lands are excep-tionally vulnerable to the ravages of this malady. An African student, who attended a British university, opened his heart to Mary Endersbee of *Crusade* magazine and poured out his lonely experience as he struggled to adapt to an alien culture:

> At home, I walk along, my eyes raised, meeting the eyes of the people coming along the road towards me—neighbors, family, friends. We call out, we greet one another. Here in Britain I walk along your streets. People's eyes do not meet mine. They look away, avoiding my glance. No one greets me, no one calls out. Everyone seems to be rushing, silent.

How deep and poignant was this man's loneli-ness! And he is representative of thousands.

A student in one university carved a pathetic question on his desk: "Why am I so lonely when there are two thousand here?" He was learning the painful lesson that there can be close physical contact without meaningful relationship.

> Yes! in the sea of life enisled,
> With echoing straits between us thrown,
> Dotting the shoreless watery wild,
> We mortal millions live *alone*.
> —Matthew Arnold, "To Marguerite"

SOLITUDE
IS NOT LONELINESS

It is nothing new to be lonely. It comes to all of us
sooner or later. . . . If we try to retreat from it, we
end in a darker hell. But if we face it, if we remember that there are a million others like us, if we
reach out and try to comfort them and not ourselves,
we find in the end that we are lonely no longer.
—Morris West, *The Devil's Advocate*

While there are points of similarity between solitude
and loneliness, it is quite wrong to equate them
without qualification. It is true that the two at times
do converge, but neither the words nor the experience are synonymous.

The word *alone* occurs frequently in the Bible,
but only in very few cases can it be equated with
loneliness. Our Lord differentiated the two concepts
when He said, "You will leave me all alone. Yet I am
not alone, for my Father is with me" (John 16:32).
The different significance of the two words has been
expressed in this way: *Loneliness* is the result of the
absence of personal intimacy or meaningful activity.
Solitude is not being in the company of others.

Loneliness is always and essentially a negative

experience, while solitude is often positive and renewing. Loneliness brings a feeling of desolation and depression that can be destructive. It tends to stifle hope and quench aspiration. Solitude can generate a sense of solitariness that is both creative and motivating. The one is involuntary, unwanted. The other is voluntary and deliberately chosen.

Isolation was the first thing that God saw was not good: "It is not good for the man to be alone" (Gen. 2:18). But there are times when the hard-pressed heart craves solitude more than anything else.

> I wish
> That I could enter in
> And close the door
> Of my small house
> To dwell alone
> As little shellfish do.
> —Mumei

Following His claim that isolation was not good for Adam, God created "a helper suitable for him." So early in human history, God indicated that mankind was made for companionship. We were created social beings, capable of sustaining loving and congenial relationships with both God and our fellow men and women. Our full creative purpose can never be realized by itself, only in association with other men and women. Because we are social creatures by nature, the absence of a friend or companion creates an emotional vacuum that can work havoc on both body and spirit.

When the late Duke of Windsor abdicated the

throne of Britain to marry the woman he loved, but who was not acceptable to the Royal Family, he went into a self-imposed exile. As a result of his own bitter experience he declared that loneliness was not simply a matter of being alone, but rather the feeling that no one really cares what happens to you. It is not necessarily caused by a set of circumstances—it is a state of mind.

Harry Sisler betrayed real insight into the inwardness of the problem when he wrote:

> The human spirit seems doomed to live alone.
> That which we share is but the threshold
> Of the habitation of our being. Still unshown
> Are the deeply hidden qualities which enfold.
> That which is truly us we don't disclose.

Being alone involves only physical separation, but being lonely includes both spiritual and psychological isolation. It produces a solitude of heart, the feeling of being cut off from others whom we should like to have as friends.

A certain degree of solitude—being alone with one's thoughts—is a normal state. It is essential to the cultivation of the inner life. We all experience times when it becomes essential to escape what Thomas Gray called "the madding crowd's ignoble strife" and engage in constructive introspection. Without such periodic physical withdrawal, the spiritual life will lack depth and freshness. In such a period of solitude we will find a welcome alternative to the rat race of modern life.

"Most of us are so engrossed in making a living," said one writer, "that we do not stop to think whether we are making a life." We need to be alone to discover and confront our real selves. A time of self-imposed solitude has often led to invaluable self-analysis and a fresh outlook on life.

Thank you, God, for making restful silence,
Loveliest of all the sounds I hear.
My ears are aching and my body tenses,
Too many sounds, too loud, too near.

CONSTRUCTIVE SOLITUDE

Periods of loneliness, if used in a ruthlessly honest manner, can equip us to help others who find themselves facing the same problem. Our Lord's frequent desire for solitude was not for the mere sake of being alone; it was primarily to enjoy communion with His Father. Then, strengthened and encouraged by that fellowship, He returned better equipped to meet the demands of the needy and lonely crowds that constantly pursued Him.

Far from being an unwelcome liability, solitude confers many fringe benefits. It is in the place of quietness that creativity flourishes, not in the hubbub of modern life. We are so constituted that while we crave intimacy with other human beings, there are times when solitude becomes imperative, especially the silence of aloneness with God, when other voices have died away. It is then we have the unique opportunity of listening unhurriedly to His "voice of gentle stillness." The enrichment that follows cannot be exaggerated, for communion with the eternal God is the most potent medium of inner fulfillment.

The need for quietness and solitude was never greater than it is today. A. W. Tozer writes in his book *Of God and Men* that some of God's children "want to discover the blessedness of spiritual aloneness," to relearn the ways of solitude and simplicity. To such he offers this counsel:

> Retire from the world each day to some private spot. . . . Stay in the secret place till the surrounding noises begin to fade out of your heart and a sense of God's presence envelopes you. Deliberately tune out the unpleasant sounds and come out of your closet determined not to hear them. Listen for the inward Voice till you learn to recognize it. . . . Learn to pray inwardly every moment. After a while you can do this even while you work.

REGAINING HEAVEN'S PERSPECTIVE

Solitude affords the needed opportunity of regaining heaven's perspective on the mysteries of life. This was the experience of Asaph the psalmist, who opens his heart and shares his perplexity in Psalm 73.

As he surveyed the world around him and observed the prosperity of the wicked people among whom he moved, he almost lost his faith. He was mystified that God should allow them to prosper and profit by their evil deeds, while often the good people appeared to have more than their share of adversity and suffering. Was God really being fair by acting that way? In the light of His seeming injustice,

Asaph had begun to wonder about the point and profit of being righteous.

James Russell Lowell might have had Asaph's grievance in mind when he wrote his well-known lines:

> Careless seems the great Avenger,
> History's pages but record
> One death-grapple in the darkness
> 'Twixt old systems and the Word.
> Truth for ever on the scaffold,
> Wrong for ever on the throne.

Hear Asaph as he pours out his complaint:

> As for me, my feet had almost slipped; I had nearly lost my foothold. For I envied the arrogant when I saw the prosperity of the wicked. They have no struggles; their bodies are healthy and strong. They are free from the burdens common to man; they are not plagued by human ills. . . . This is what the wicked are like—always carefree, they increase in wealth. Surely in vain have I kept my heart pure . . . . When I tried to understand all this, it was oppressive to me *till I entered the sanctuary of God; then I understood* . . . (Ps. 73:2–5, 12–13, 16–17; *italics mine*).

It was not until he repaired to the silence of the sanctuary of God that heaven's perspective once again gained the ascendancy and he found a fresh foothold for his faith. It was there that the truth enshrined in Lowell's following lines gripped his soul:

> Yet that scaffold sways the future,
> And behind the dim unknown
> Standeth God within the shadows,
> Keeping watch above His own.

Habakkuk the prophet was equally mystified, and for the same reason as Asaph, as he looked at the world around him from his lonely watchtower:

> How long, O Lord, must I call for help, but you do not listen? Or cry out to you, "Violence!" but you do not save? Why do you make me look at injustice? Why do you tolerate wrong? (Hab. 1:2–3).

In his reflection on this passage in *Life of Faith* magazine, W. S. Hooton writes, "Like many today [Habakkuk] seems to have found it difficult to reconcile with the divine government the triumphs of the wicked and treacherous over those who, whatever their sins, were not so laden with guilt. The sins of God's people had called for correction (1:12), and the prophet knew where their refuge was to be found."

Where did he find the answer to his perplexity? In his watchtower, when he listened for the voice of God.

In the rush of our pressured lives it is easy to allow the world to dictate our agenda, to squeeze us into its mold, while we ourselves are unconscious of the subtle erosion of our own standards and values. Jesus did not allow even the tragic need and suffering of the masses to rob Him of those precious times of quiet. They were sacred oases in the desert of human sin.

He identified Himself so thoroughly with our humanity that He experienced acute loneliness— one of the sinless infirmities that He voluntarily assumed at the Incarnation. It was no surprise to Him when His disciples all forsook Him and fled. Had He not already forewarned them of that danger? And they deserted Him in His hour of greatest need. But in that darkest hour of His loneliness, He confessed His unshaken confidence in His Father's abiding presence:

> You will leave me all alone. *Yet I am not alone, for my Father is with me* (John 16:32; *italics mine*).

This joyous fact more than compensated for the absence of human companionship. He knew the ultimate panacea for loneliness, and so may we.

Let the desolate soul take comfort from the fact that God is just as present with His lonely children today as He was with His Son. But it is only as we believe and appropriate that fact that we will enjoy the blessing and benefit of His conscious presence.

Out of his rich experience of walking with God, Thomas à Kempis gave this advice concerning the value of solitude:

> Watch for good times to retreat into your-

self. Frequently meditate on how good God is to you. Skip the tricky questions. Read things which move your heart. If you will stop gossiping and chattering, you will find plenty of time for helpful meditation.

You will find in your closet of prayer what you frequently lose when you are out in the world. The more you visit it, the more you will want to return. But the more you avoid it, the harder it will be to come back.

TRANSFORMING SOLITUDE

"So Jacob was left alone" (Gen. 32:24). These words have a plaintive ring about them. But in the encounter that ensued, Jacob discovered to his great surprise that he was alone with the very God who, for two decades, had been pursuing him with undiscouraged ardor, with the sole purpose of blessing him. And now he had painted himself into a corner.

To soften up the brother whom he had so shamefully defrauded, Jacob had sent on ahead his wife, children, and flocks, together with lavish presents for Esau. And now he was all alone!

How he dreaded the hour of confrontation with his brother! Little did he dream that this unplanned hour of solitude would be fraught with unimagined blessing. He had to learn that God never gives up in His desire to bless his erring children.

> Come O Thou Traveler unknown,
> Whom still I hold, but cannot see;
> My company before is gone,

And I am left alone with Thee:
With Thee all night I mean to stay,
And wrestle till the break of day.
                    —Charles Wesley

But the words *left alone* can hold different connotations to different people. For some they spell longed-for rest and quietness, for others only aching loneliness. To be left alone without God is hell. But to be left alone with God is a foretaste of heaven.

It was only when Jacob the deceiver was shut up alone with God that he was transformed into Israel the prince, who now had power with God and man. What marvelous grace on God's part! One could conceive of our generous God granting him the privilege of having influence with his fellow men. This would be an incredible expression of divine forgiveness and restoration. But to have power with God? Only a God as great and as gracious as our God could have conceived such an act of love and grace.

Lame as I am, I take the prey,
Hell, earth and sin with ease o'ercome,
I leap for joy, pursue my way,
And as a bounding hart fly home,
Through all eternity to prove
Thy nature and Thy name is love.
                    —Charles Wesley

NO AGE-GROUP IS IMMUNE

Since my youth, O God, you have taught me, and to
this day I declare your marvelous deeds. Even when
I am old and gray, do not forsake me, O God, till I
declare your power to the next generation, your
might to all who are to come.
—Psalm 71:17–18

In his unique way, Shakespeare has depicted in *The
Seven Ages of Man* the distinctive character traits of
the individual at each stage of life. A similar pro-
gression may be seen in man's spiritual pilgrimage.
Each stage of life's ongoing development has its own
peculiar characteristics. Unfortunately it is also true
that from childhood to old age, loneliness is present
and tends to assume a different form in each era of
life. No age-bracket is immune from its ravages.

Young children can experience loneliness very
early in life. In his book *Fear of Love,* Ira J. Tanner
says, "Loneliness has its beginning in childhood,
sometime between the ages of one and three. It is a
root condition of life, and it is during these post-
embryonic years that we first begin to experience
doubt as to our self-worth."

Childish emotions are doubtless more fleeting

than those of adults, but to the child they are painfully real at the time. The shy child, for example, suffers agonies when separated from her mother on the first day of school. In the same way the backward or unpopular child, the one with some physical deformity, will feel rejected, left out, unwanted.

Other children are lonely because their parents spend so little time with them, or are insensitive to their need of affection. The greatly reduced time two working parents are able to spend with their children creates an emotional vacuum in their children's hearts.

With some sensitive children, misunderstandings or fear of punishment may cause them to take refuge in withdrawal, or to live in a world of fantasy. One nine-year-old boy, for instance, was playing with his friends recently when accidentally he started a fire that resulted in some damage. Because he had been warned by his mother not to play with matches, he was afraid to own up to his involvement.

When his mother asked him if he had been involved, he flatly denied it. However, from his subsequent withdrawn behavior his parents were convinced that he had played some part in the fire. Again he steadfastly denied it. But when his mother assured him that if he had started the fire and confessed it, he would not be punished, he broke down and acknowledged his part in the incident. It was a very relieved little boy who burst out of the icehouse of loneliness that his fear had erected.

A recent survey reveals that loneliness is the biggest problem confronting teenagers today. In *The Untapped Resource*, Ida Nell Holloway confirms this when she reports that adolescents and young adults tend to be even more acutely lonely than do the elderly. This springs, in part, from the desperate need they feel to be socially accepted, especially by their peers. They have reached the in-between stage when they feel identity with neither child nor adult. As a result they are uncertain how to discover a niche into which they can fit comfortably.

Naturally enough they want to be individuals in their own right. I remember my son telling me that in his early adolescence he did not want to be known merely as my son, he wanted to be himself—a perfectly natural stage of development.

It is at this point that many young people become estranged from their parents and throw off restraint. In their loneliness they hunger for understanding and acceptance. If this is not extended to them at home, they seek it elsewhere, sometimes in questionable places.

Excessive noise and frenzied activity seem to be an essential element in contemporary adolescent behavior patterns. Adults do not always appreciate the result, and when objection is taken to the excesses, the young person feels rejected and disapproved and retreats into his loneliness.

All these factors combine to produce an acute loneliness that sometimes finds expression in antisocial behavior. It is not surprising, therefore, that the suicide rate among adolescents has doubled in recent years.

In his book *Lonely, But Never Alone*, Nicky Cruz concluded, "Although some suicides are drug-induced, most youthful suicides or attempted suicides have a history of unhappiness, fears, or loneliness behind them. Those who look to suicide as a solution already feel alone in the world."

In their rebellion against parental restrictions, some young people try to drown their loneliness in alcohol or drugs or by spurning the standards and culture of their family in both dress and behavior. In this way they hope to find acceptance with a more congenial group, even though they are "way out." It is among these young people that the greatest problems of law enforcement are encountered.

The only child faces yet another type of loneliness. To ward off its pangs, he often withdraws into a world of fantasy. If he does not happen to be creative or imaginative, able to make his own amusement, he finds himself living largely in an adult world. This in turn makes it more difficult for him to form easy relationships with his peers in the world of reality.

The adopted child who is aware of that fact faces yet another set of problems. He has to deal with that peculiar type of loneliness that is generated by a lack of identity. Who are his parents? Why did they abandon him? Why was he not wanted? Is he illegitimate? Kind though the adoptive parents may be, the often unanswered questions leave their mark on a sensitive and lonely heart.

Older people are expected to be lonely! But it is a mistake to lump them all together and equate old age with loneliness. Research discloses that many old people fare much better in this respect than do their younger counterparts. For this there are valid reasons. Loneliness usually takes young people by surprise. Older people, on the other hand, expect some degree of loneliness.

As times passes they discover that most of their contemporaries are having somewhat parallel experiences, and so they are more likely to take their condition philosophically. These are not in the majority, however. A greater number of the aged are desperately lonely. For them life seems to hold little meaning, especially if they are housebound. They feel neither needed nor wanted, and this is one of the most poignant aspects of old age. Everyone wants to feel needed.

Mother Teresa of Calcutta has spent her life working among the poor and lepers of that tragic city. In accepting the 1979 Nobel Prize, which she was awarded for her amazing sacrificial service, she said that she had come more and more to realize that it is being unwanted that is the worst disease any human being can ever experience. Disease of the spirit is more serious than disease of the body.

For many elderly people—especially men—television is most important, for it helps pass the weary, pointless hours less monotonously. But at best it is a one-way street. It demands no response. It requires only passive observation. And the old saying proves too true: Impression without expression brings depression.

Those confined in nursing homes are lonely because they are separated from friends and relatives, sometimes in an environment that is far from congenial. Because many of their companions are well advanced along the road to senility, stimulating conversation is rare.

Not long ago I was having lunch with a friend who had entered her second century. I was amused when she took me by the arm and led me away. "Come and let us have some intelligent conversation," she said. "I hardly ever have sensible conversation with the others in the nursing home." To those whose powers are still sharp and functioning, such an atmosphere must be depressing.

There are few for whom the crisis of retirement, whether voluntary or enforced, does not create some degree of emotional upheaval. The loss of congenial companionship and status that usually accompanies retirement tends to generate a loss of self-worth as well. A decreasing contact with familiar society can leave the retiree without a stimulating goal or congenial occupation. The cheerful chitchat enjoyed with business associates or workmates is sorely missed, and life descends into dull monotony.

For the busy mother, a new crisis is reached when the last child leaves the nest. This can be for her just as traumatic an experience as her husband's retirement from business life is to him. The once noisily happy home suddenly becomes a somber vacuum. Life loses its significance and mothers of adult children lose their motivation. Unless she can find some meaningful substitute activity, loneliness will inevitably take over. Fortunately, it is often at this stage of life that the advent of grandchildren breaks the pattern.

For the Christian, retirement should be viewed as a divinely-given and valuable opportunity for new adventure and achievement. The best days do not all lie in the past. The years of lifted responsibility should be regarded only as a junction, not a terminus, an exciting new beginning, even a new career. It has proved to be so in many cases.

> While closing days leave something to do,
> Some deeper truth to learn, some gift to gain,
> Let me with cheerful mind my path pursue,
> And thankful, glean the fragments that remain.
> —T. D. Bernard

But not everyone embraces such an outlook. Contrast that optimistic outlook on life's closing days with that which Lord Byron depicts in his *Childe Harold:*

> What is the worst of foes that wait on age?
> What stamps the wrinkle deeper on the brow?
> To view each loved one blotted from life's page,
> And be as I am now.

But older people or retirees need not feel that their days of significant contribution are in the past. There is no need for them to resign themselves to lonely purposelessness. Though they may be less active physically than before, there is no reason why their closing years should not be even more influential in another way. Through the years they have acquired a store of wisdom and experience that they can share with the rising generation.

Longfellow recognized the possibility of continuing fruitfulness in old age when he wrote:

For age is opportunity, no less
Than youth itself, though in another dress;
And as the evening twilight fades away,
The sky is filled with stars
Invisible by day.

4

THE NUCLEAR FAMILY

More people are feeling lonely. Their lives consist of
proximity without presence, relationship without
contact, and familiarity without feelings.
—Tim Timmons, *Loneliness Is Not a Disease*

The changes in current social structures have made
us more vulnerable to loneliness than was the case
in earlier years. As recently as last century, the
great majority of homes were multigenerational.
Both social functions and religious activity had their
focus in the home. Children were born there, with
friends and relatives around the expectant mother—
a far cry from the sterile modern hospital. Deaths
occurred there, and funerals were conducted from
the family home, not from the commercial funeral
home.

While this was not without its problems, the
result of the inevitably close interaction was to
make the family a well-integrated unit, whose members laughed and cried, worked and played
together—again a far cry from the experience of
today's so-called nuclear family.

Even in such a close-knit community it was possible for family members to be painfully lonely. But

the chances were against it. Today the whole picture is reversed. Instead of being the center of family life, the home has become, in the main, a point of departure—to school, to work, to sport, to social activity, to church.

Today's nuclear family, consisting of father, mother, and one or two children, has replaced the multigenerational family of the last century. This radical social change carries within itself the seeds of its own desolation; for as the current generation is proving, present sociological conditions are a fertile plot for acute loneliness.

Imagine the loneliness of the single child now permitted to Chinese parents. In their efforts to contain the population explosion, Chinese authorities have erased two words from their vocabulary—brother and sister. Most Chinese children of the recent generation have neither.

The ever-increasing mobility and restlessness of our society, resulting from the prevalence of auto and air travel, tends to increase the problem. Some estimate that in many communities more than one family in five changes its location every year. Add to this the fact that because of economic conditions a diminishing number of families now own their own home, and we have a situation that prohibits families from putting down deep roots. There is also an industrial flow that causes people to keep moving in the hope of gaining stability and financial security in more congenial circumstances.

In many countries, immigration and the influx of refugees and foreign seasonal workers add another dimension and increase the community of the lonely. The ethnic mix, with its consequent linguistic confusion, constitutes another isolating factor. Many of the student children of the first generation of immigrants, who have been torn from their own familiar culture, find the adjustment extremely painful.

In the bustling republic of Singapore, almost three-quarters of the population live in small apartments in towering high-rise buildings. This is the pattern of living that is emerging in the burgeoning cities of many developing nations.

This congested mode of communal living, however, discourages the development of warm and enduring relationships with other families in the complex. Few people get to know their fellow tenants in more than a casual manner. Families live in isolation, and the prevalent mood of restlessness makes it easy to pack up and move to another location, which usually proves equally lonely. The lifestyle of those who live in apartments inhibits the formation of those close relationships so essential to the wholesome development of a growing family.

The rapid acceleration of urbanization in most countries of the world necessarily involves the severing of agelong family ties, leaving behind the familiar culture and moving into a large, impersonal, and unwelcoming city to face an unknown future. It takes no vivid imagination to envision the trauma of such a situation.

The latest demographic reports reveal that there are now three hundred cities of more than one million inhabitants, and the sobering fact is that the majority of these cities are in the economically distressed developing countries, which are least able to cope with the problems that result from overpopulation. For many who leave their rural situations this means a loss of identity, roots.

Because of economic necessity, both parents in the majority of urban families are at work, a condition that has become the norm, not the exception. This results in a minimum amount of time families can spend together in relaxed fun and fellowship. Youth centers and sports activities claim much of the free time of young people, and each member of the family spends far more time away from home, even in leisure hours.

TELEVISION AND TODAY'S FAMILY

A further word on the impact of television on the family is appropriate, for there is no doubt that it has played a significant part in producing loneliness. It has changed the face of society, and on the whole, it has had a subtly harmful effect on family togetherness. Ordinary conversation between family members is reduced to a minimum. Children cease to communicate freely with parents, sitting instead with eyes glued to the fascinating box. Attempts to limit viewing time or monitor programs are either futile or at least unpleasant.

The vast impact of television on the children of our times is revealed by the fact that when the average child turns eighteen years of age, he or she will have spent more than twenty-two thousand viewing hours in the lonely world of TV.

A. C. Nielsen Co., the research firm whose ratings determine the fate of America's television pro-

gramming, provide these startling facts concerning
the influence of the media on home and family. During the 1987–88 season, the average American
household watched TV for an estimated time of four
and one-half hours a day.

Vladimir Kosma Zworykin, the Russian-born
inventor of television, said on his ninety-first birthday, "I would never let my children even come close
to this thing."

Neil Postman, professor of communications at
New York University, said in a *U.S. News & World
Report* interview that TV, as a curriculum, molds the
intelligence and character of youth far more than
formal schooling. How important, then, that they
view the right programs.

Malcolm Muggeridge, who was at one time
Britain's foremost television interviewer, caustically
expressed his view of the effect of television on family and community:

> Consider our excessive and obsessive tele-
> viewing. The average modern man looks at
> television for four hours every day, which
> means that he spends ten years of his life
> looking into the television screen; some-
> thing that precludes reading, conversation,
> and other exercises in literacy.
> —*The End of Christendom*

Even the valuable and interesting newscasts
have a minus as well as a plus. NBC news commen-
tator John Chancellor pointed out that the difference between viewing TV newscasts and reading a

newspaper is enormous. A man reading his newspaper can be his own editor. But with TV, you have either to take it, or turn it off.

So even after making generous allowance for the undoubted beneficial aspects of TV, we must conclude that it is responsible for a growing degree of isolation and consequent loneliness, even within the family.

VIOLENCE, INTIMACY, AND THE MODERN FAMILY

But one can be very lonely even in the midst of the family circle. The sharp increase reported in family violence indicates that there is significantly less wholesome communication, but more isolation and estrangement, than in earlier days. Then, it was the family that provided stability and afforded the basic environment for the normal development of personality. Now, on the contrary, violence within the family is emerging as a major source of crime. Refuges for battered wives and children have become the order of the day.

It is reported that twenty percent of police deaths in the U.S. are attributed to police intervention in family disputes. The ultimate effect of this violence on the children, who learn their behavior patterns in the home, is to perpetuate those patterns in the homes of the next generation. This is no longer theory but established fact.

One would have expected the home to be the place of deepest intimacy—and in many cases it is. But too often it has degenerated into a place of shattered ideals and blasted hopes. Instead of love, there are loneliness and isolation.

One hopeful sign in an otherwise bleak picture is the increased attention being paid by both church and state to the importance of the family in the life of the nation. In both circles, increasing numbers of well-qualified and caring professional people are being assigned to work in this vastly important segment of the community.

THE EFFECTS OF
LONELINESS ON HEALTH

A nine-year study by researchers at the University of California shows that loneliness has a greater impact on the death rate than smoking, drinking, eating, or exercise. The study found that people without spouses or friends had a death rate twice as high as those with social ties.
—ABC News

Loneliness is usually considered a matter of the emotions, and indeed it is. But in its acute and unrelieved form its effects are not confined to the emotions. Specialists in both mental and emotional health assert that it can induce most painful and even harmful physical repercussions, as many sufferers have learned to their dismay.

For this reason alone it must be viewed as a serious health hazard. One eminent specialist advanced the opinion that there is a biological basis for our need to form close human relationships, and added that if we fail to do this we are putting our health at risk. So it is a matter of urgency that the lonely person diligently seeks to analyze its cause and apply the appropriate remedy.

The physiological effects vary with the individual, since the constitution of each person is unique. Migraine, exhaustion, or apathy are common side effects. Eating habits may be affected, or obesity may result from overeating in the search for some compensating influence for the inner ache. In some cases sexual desire is greatly decreased or totally inhibited. If the lonely condition is unduly prolonged or excessive, it can produce a significant change in personality.

Profound psychological effects may also be induced. Since emotion plays such a dominant role in the whole of life, undue suppression of the emotions can have harmful psychological results. The better course is to find some satisfying outlet for them—even tears—than to keep them suppressed. The macho image that some men try to display can be seriously counterproductive in this respect.

It is an understandable though unhelpful tendency of lonely persons to take refuge by withdrawing into themselves rather than seeking the company of others. This reaction often has its rise in a fear that in any close relationship some failure or other personality defect may surface, bringing the relationship to an untimely end. Although they are all the time craving friendship, this fear causes lonely individuals to keep their true selves concealed. This, in turn, makes it difficult for them to approach others first and equally difficult for others to make a friendly advance.

The prominent psychiatrist William Glasser makes this surprising assertion in his book *The Identity Society*:

All symptoms, whether psychological or psychosomatic, and all aggressive, irrational behavior are products of loneliness and are companions to the lonely, suffering people who struggle for an identity, but do not succeed. Instead, they identify themselves as failures.

No less serious are the inroads of loneliness made on family life. The absence of stable foundations for family life creates an atmosphere of insecurity and uncertainty that only worsens the condition. Loneliness causes some to lash out in violent speech or action. Rather than becoming depressed as do others in like cases, these lonely souls get angry and express their frustrations in destructive activity.

Alcohol and drug addiction are often symptoms of unchecked loneliness. But they are not the real malady. When a lonely person fails to find acceptance in normal society, he or she may try this escape route, which at first promises so much, but in the end delivers so little and ends in a depressing cul-de-sac.

Then, too, there is a vital connection between loneliness and sickness. People overtaken by serious illness are compelled to spend much time alone. They are frequently taken by surprise with such an event and are therefore unprepared to meet the crisis. The stark contrast between the liberty enjoyed by friends and loved ones and their own separation from the normal pursuits of life is often a painful experience.

If the sick person is confined to a hospital or

nursing home, visiting hours are limited, and even where they are more generous, friends do not have unlimited time for visitation. When loneliness is added to the pain of the illness, they can weigh on the spirits of even the most buoyant patient.

Hospital chaplains report that in the course of their visitation they meet many patients who have no friends, no one to visit and cheer them from year to year. To such sufferers loneliness is inevitable and corrosive. It is small wonder if their thoughts turn inwards in self-pity and they succumb to bitterness.

Chronic illness and infirmity always lead to a measure of isolation. With the passage of time, friends move away or drop off for one reason or another. In larger cities the distance one must travel is another limiting factor. So visitors become less frequent.

But there is no need for a sickbed to become a prison. It is possible for our minds and imaginations to enrich our solitude. The Christian who knows the comfort of the Scriptures, and who maintains a vital and outgoing prayer life, will find in those exercises a satisfying panacea for his own need. He can rove the world in his prayers and thus contribute to the fulfillment of Christ's Great Commission.

A glowing example of one who rose above her confining surroundings is that of Madame Jeanne de la Mothe Guyon, a member of the French nobility who was imprisoned in the infamous Bastille for fifteen years during the French Revolution.

In spite of the atrocious conditions in which she found herself, so great was her delight in God that her spirit soared far above her prison walls. She said the stones in her prison walls shone like rubies. Triumphant in spirit, she penned these verses:

A little bird am I.
Shut out from fields of air,
Yet in my cage I sit and sing
To Him who placed me there!
Well pleased a prisoner to be,
Because, my God, it pleaseth Thee.

Naught else have I to do,
I sing the whole day long,
And He whom most I love to please
Doth listen to my song.
He caught and bound my wandering wing,
And still He loves to hear me sing.

My cage confines me round,
Abroad I cannot soar,
But though my wing is closely bound
My heart's at liberty.
My prison walls cannot control
The flight, the freedom of the soul.

O it is good to soar
These bolts and bars above,
To Him whose purpose I adore,
Whose providence I love,
And in Thy mighty will to find
The joy and freedom of the mind.

Like that confining prison, a sickbed can be transformed into a throne and become a center of ministry and salvation, as the following incident reveals:

In 1939 it was my privilege to visit one of God's great noblewomen, Hannah Higgens of Melbourne, Australia. For sixty-nine of her eighty-two years she had been in constant pain as the result of a progressive bone disease that ultimately required the amputation of both arms and legs. Yet in her "cage" she would "sit and sing to Him who placed her there." She named her cottage "Gladwish." And for forty-three years she lived in one room.

How easy it would have been for her to give up the struggle and relapse into an orgy of self-pity. Instead, she accepted her limitations and acted on her God-given ministry to share with other invalids the love and comfort of God that had been her portion.

She had an attachment fixed to the stump of her right arm that enabled her to write with a fountain pen. It takes little imagination to understand the physical effort she had to exert when writing, since she had to use her whole body to form each character. As I write, I have before me one of her letters in the almost flawless script she learned to write.

Hannah's little room became a place of pilgrimmage for people from all over the world. From it went thousands of letters to visitors and fellow sufferers worldwide, which produced a rich harvest of blessing. The walls of her room were covered with photographs of correspondents to whom she had ministered and in many cases had led to the Lord. Of her it could be truly said that she turned her trouble into treasure and her sorrow into song.

Hazel Gillanders, writing in *New Life* magazine, records these sentiments of Miss Higgens:

"I have so much to be thankful for, so many mercies," she wrote. "I have often tried to count them but it is impossible. They are innumerable. Although I am deprived of health and strength and my limbs, Jesus is far more precious than ever. . . . I am so often asked if I do not find the time long. I do not, and I can truthfully say that I never feel lonely."

Who can measure the glory and joy this valiant sufferer brought to the heart of God, or the streams of blessing that flowed around the world from that humble room?

I recently received a letter from a friend in which he says the following:

While walking in the desert, Moses discovered a bush on fire. Amazingly, the bush was not burning up, so Moses drew closer to see why. Then God spoke to him out of the burning bush. It was not unusual to see a bush burning; it is unusual that the bush was not consumed. It's not unusual to see people hit by fiery trials; it's remarkable when they are not consumed by them. And God often speaks to onlookers through one in the midst of trial.

6

SINGLE, BUT NOT LONELY

It is good for a man not to marry....
Now to the unmarried and the widows I say:
It is good for them to stay unmarried, as I am....
Now about virgins:... I think that it is good
for you to remain as you are.
—1 Corinthians 7:1, 8, 25–26

"I live alone, and yet I am never lonely. Why should I be lonely when I have God?" These words were spoken by a woman ninety years old, in precarious health, and with few worldly goods. She exemplifies the fact that singleness need not be equated with loneliness.

Each generation creates its own name for different categories of people. "Teenagers" and "yuppies" are widely used today. But in this half of the twentieth century, two new categories have emerged—"singles" and "solo parents." Of course they have always been with us, but never in the proportions they have reached today. Either by choice or by force of circumstances, an increasing number of people are living alone.

The prevalence of divorce and the acceptance of homosexuality as an alternative lifestyle have added dramatically to the number of singles. So significant is this shift in our culture that it has disturbed the whole social structure and created a need for major changes in legislation.

The emergence of a high-technology society and the pressures of financial need have influenced more women to focus on their careers, rather than on home and family as before. The comparative affluence enjoyed in many western nations tends to encourage the growth of the single lifestyle.

One report contends that the number of American citizens living alone increased by 385 percent between the years 1971–81. The result is that the number of children living with one parent has also greatly increased. Almost one person in three lives alone. A comparable trend, although to a somewhat lesser extent, is occurring in other developed countries.

The single woman is especially prone to suffer from acute loneliness as she sees her peers marrying and establishing homes and families of their own. Many yearn deeply for the fulfillment of their God-given capacity for motherhood. In a world that is geared largely to the married set, she is tempted to feel like a misfit, undesirable. But our society is adapting to this situation.

SINGLENESS AND MISSIONS

When thinking of singleness, we should not overlook the fact that Jesus and Paul found satisfaction and fulfillment in the single state. In fact, some of the world's greatest saints, both men and women, have been single.

The mission fields of the world would be greatly undone were it not for the magnificent contribution of single women—a contribution that fortunately continues.

A striking example of the way in which a group of single women found fulfillment while single occurred in the interior of China. Hudson Taylor, founder of the China Inland Mission (now Overseas Missionary Fellowship), was a pioneer in several areas of missionary work. It was he who first encouraged lay persons to undertake missionary work. It was he, too, who first engaged single women in pioneering new areas in China. In 1885 the mission opened centers on the populous Kwang Sin River, and because there were no men available for the task, the work was conducted entirely by single women.

Thirty-two years later there was a complete chain of ten central stations, sixty outstations, over two thousand church members, and many more people interested in spiritual matters. These and other single women who joined them were still the only foreign missionaries alongside the national pastors they had trained. No one could say that they had not found fulfillment, even though single.

PAUL'S VIEWPOINT

In his classic treatment of the subject of the unmarried or the widowed, Paul repeated three times the assertion that "it is good to be [or remain] unmarried." Here are his statements:

> *It is good* for a man not to marry. . . . Now to the unmarried and the widows I say: *It is*

> *good* for them to stay unmarried, as I am. . . .
> Now about virgins: I have no command
> from the Lord, but I give a judgment . . . .
> *Because of the present crisis,* I think that *it
> is good* for you to remain as you are. . . . Are
> you unmarried? Do not look for a wife (1
> Cor. 7:1, 8, 25–27; *italics mine*).

In the first two verses Paul makes it clear that
he is writing by command of the Lord. In the third
passage he states that it is an expression of his sanc-
tified judgment concerning the wisdom of getting
married, in view of the current critical political situation. In other words, he is not laying down a universal prohibition for all time.

He does not indicate the nature of the crisis, but
in those turbulent days in the Roman Empire, crises
were common. He apparently considered the exist-
ing crisis so serious that he believed the wiser
course for the unmarried would be to remain single
until the crisis was resolved.

CHRIST'S TEACHING

Our Lord, too, made an important pronouncement
on the subject, which gives assurance that singleness can be both honorable and praiseworthy.

> For some are eunuchs because they were
> born that way; others were made that way
> by men; and others have renounced mar-
> riage because of the kingdom of heaven.
> The one who can accept this should accept
> it (Matt. 19:12).

The implication is plain. There are some who are so disciplined and motivated that they choose singleness so that they may better give undistracted service to the Lord and their fellowmen.

Jesus did not make this mandatory, but optional. Not everyone can ascend to such a disciplined lifestyle. But we must acknowledge that the church and the world owe much to those who have deliberately chosen this sacrificial course.

So, from the teaching of both Christ and Paul we learn that neither regarded the single state as second best. Nor should single people consider themselves in any sense inferior or underprivileged. Paul reinforced this view when he wrote:

I wish that all men were as I am. But each man has his own gift from God; one has this gift [the gift of being married], another has that [the gift of being single] (1 Cor. 7:7).

But not all single people are able to regard their state in that light! It is not unnatural for them to compare their lot with that of their contemporaries who, after work, return to a welcoming home and family, and not to an empty apartment.

Sometimes circumstances make it either inadvisable or impossible to marry. For others the opportunity of marriage has not come their way; or a promising relationship has not materialized. In such cases, the well-worn saying stands true: "In acceptance lies peace."

On one occasion I heard a single missionary in her early thirties give her testimony before leaving for her second furlough. She told frankly of her longing for a life partner and admitted what a struggle it had been for her to face the continuing loneliness of single life on the mission field.

When furlough time came, she decided that she must realistically face and settle the matter once and for all. She said to herself: "Well, it appears you're 'on the shelf.' No one seems to be dying to marry you, in spite of your prayers. You might as well accept that as final and get on with your job."

Once she had definitely faced and accepted the fact of her singleness as being God's good and perfect will for her, the tumult subsided and her heart was at peace. She testified that she was going home full of joy and peace, even though she was permanently "on the shelf."

But that was not the end of the story. Not long after her return to the field, to her joy and surprise she discovered that someone was "dying to marry her." Today she and her husband are making a valuable contribution to the kingdom of God in Asia.

Things do not always work out so happily, but notice that once she had accepted the fact of her singleness—instead of rebelling and fighting against it—the dove of peace alighted on her heart. But even if no offer of marriage had come to her, the peace of God would have ousted the old loneliness, and she would have proved the truth of Romans 12:2 that the will of God is "good, pleasing and perfect." She would be able to sing with Tersteegen:

> Thou sweet, beloved will of God,
> My anchor ground, my fortress hill,

My spirit's silent, fair abode,
In Thee I hide me and am still.

Upon God's will I lay me down,
As child upon its mother's breast;
No silken couch, nor softest bed
Could ever give me such deep rest.

Thy wonderful, grand will, my God,
With triumph now I make it mine,
And faith shall cry a joyous, Yes!
To every dear command of Thine.

THE ADVANTAGES OF SINGLENESS

With so many marriages ending in the divorce court, the loneliness that engulfs the parties to these broken marriages is probably more acute than that of the unmarried person. For the divorcee there are in addition a host of complicating factors, especially where children are involved. Single bliss can be preferable to marital misery.

In the past, people typically thought and taught that the married state was God's ideal for men and women. There is no question that it is the normal state, but in our contemporary world this ideal cannot be realized because there are statistically not enough men to go around! Inevitably some women must remain single.

If the single state is God's will for some, both men and women, even though marriage might be preferred, that will is nevertheless "good, pleasing and perfect" (Rom. 12:2). The converse is also true—anything other than the will of God is bad, displeasing, and imperfect. Therefore, because His will is acceptable, it should be accepted, adapted to, and adorned.

Philip the evangelist was blessed with four unmarried daughters (Acts 21:8–9). Their singleness did not prevent them from serving as prophetesses and exercising a fruitful and satisfying ministry. They were highly esteemed in the early church. Indeed, in writing of them, Eusebius, one of the church fathers, described them as "mighty luminaries in the early church."

This should surely encourage other single women who are not sure of their status in Christian work. The ministry of Philip's daughters was much more than getting cups of tea for the men. And down the centuries devoted single women have had a similar invaluable ministry. The service of Henrietta Mears of California, for example, was a dominant factor in the lives of over one hundred of America's great Christian leaders, like Bill Bright and Howard Hendricks.

A single woman is free to establish close ties with other single people of all ages, as well as with families. She has abundant scope for her homemaking instincts and exercising her aesthetic tastes. She can extend imaginative hospitality to the lonely and homeless. If she has her own home, she can use it in the interests of the kingdom.

Although they have no children of their own, single women have love to give away, and they can lavish their affection on other people's children. And when affection is given, it is usually reciprocated.

A missionary who was nearing her seventieth birthday once said to me: "Do you know one of the first questions I am going to ask the Lord when I get to heaven?"

"No," I replied.

"I am going to ask Him why He didn't give me a husband. I wanted a husband badly, and I would have made him a good wife!"

Though she never received the answer here, God's denial did not sour her or make her resentful and bitter. Instead, she poured the wealth of affection she would have lavished on her husband and family into the lives of thousands of children in China and Britain, for the Lord gave her a unique ministry to children.

When she died a few years ago, there were no doubt hundreds on the other side waiting to welcome her. She found her rest in accepting the Lord's assurance: "You do not realize now what I am doing, but later you will understand" (John 13:7).

So singleness can be activated for God and made spiritually productive. Remember the ninth beatitude: "It is more blessed to give than to receive" (Acts 20:35). Therein lies the secret to overcoming loneliness in the single state.

7

THE DESOLATION OF BEREAVEMENT

Let sorrow do its work,
Come grief or pain
Sweet are thy messengers,
Sweet their refrain;
When they can sing with me
More love O Christ to Thee,
More love to Thee.
—Elizabeth Prentiss

One of the most prolific creators of loneliness is the natural grief and sorrow that accompany bereavement. In the early stages of that shattering experience, the sense of loss of the loved one is so pervasive that the grieving person cannot believe the sun will ever shine again. It seems quite outside the bounds of possibility that one could ever again face life with any semblance of enjoyment.

Elisabeth Elliott, whose husband was murdered by the Auca Indians of Ecuador, to whom he had gone with the gospel, describes in poignant words her earliest reactions to the unexpected experience of bereavement. The sentiments she expresses have a familiar ring to those who have trodden the same path:

> Silent, swift, implacable, the Scythe has swept by, and we are left. . . . The mail comes, the phone rings, Wednesday gives place to Thursday, and this week to next week. You have to keep on getting up in the morning and comb your hair (for whom?), eating breakfast (remember to get out only one egg now), making the bed (who cares?).

The poignancy of the unaccustomed aloneness lies in the absence of someone to love, to care for, to talk things over with, and to serve. Someone to join in the decision-making process; someone with whom to share life's joys and laughter, life's pains and sorrows; someone with whom to revel in new and exciting discoveries in God's Word and God's world. We sorrow alone and are inclined to think, mistakenly of course, that no one has felt or could feel the intensity of the pangs of loneliness and sorrow as we do.

In the aftermath of his dearly loved wife Sarah's death, the veteran Southern preacher Vance Havner wrote these words in a *Moody Monthly* article titled "Sarah Is Gone." They will strike a responsive chord in the hearts of those recently bereaved.

> Again and again I find myself saying, "Sarah is gone!" Gone with her are a thousand other precious things that made the past so delightful. Gone is the anticipation of returning home to be greeted at the

apartment door, or at the airport. Gone is the thrill of hearing her voice at the other end of the telephone, and the cheery, "Hey, honey!" Gone are those daily airmail letters in the mail box. . . . Gone is that lovely face in the congregation, smiling at jokes she has heard me tell countless times. Gone— and the chilling, numbing awareness that it can never be again. All these years I have traveled, but never has loneliness descended on me as now. I find myself instinctively, subconsciously, looking around as though my dear Sarah ought to be somewhere nearby, reading a magazine, just waiting to be happy with me. I miss her dreadfully, but I cannot wish her back. Rather, I mend my step, and hasten on to overtake her.

GRIEF SHOULD BE ACCEPTED AND EXPRESSED

Sooner or later grief must be accepted as inevitable. We must realistically face the fact that, in the ordinary course of events, one partner in every marriage can expect to travel the last lap of the race alone. Some of our contemporaries will die before us. But the clock of life does not stop with the death of a loved partner or friend—it must go on, and so must we.

> Life must go on
> And the dead be forgotten;
> Life must go on
> Though good men die;
> Anne, eat your breakfast;

> Dan, take your medicine!
> Life must go on,
> I just forget why.
> —Edna St. Vincent Millay

The important fact is, however, that we can and do choose the manner in which we finish our own race. We are not the playthings of a relentless Fate.

"Sorrow does color life, doesn't it?" said a friend to another who had recently suffered bereavement. "Yes, indeed it does," was the reply, "But I intend to choose the colors." What colors will you choose?

I recently received a letter from a friend who had lost his wife. It was written in the early stages of his grief. " 'Oh for the touch of a vanished hand, and the sound of a voice that is still' is a quotation that had little significance for me until the finger of God touched my dear wife. I was left in the desolation and silence of living alone. However, there is no cessation from living, despite the changed conditions and the altered rhythm to which it is hard to adjust. 'My grace is sufficient' is a precious promise that enables one to go on."

In the early stages of bereavement, although we may be familiar with the textbook answers and the remedies prescribed by loving friends for the alleviation of our grief, while we may give intellectual assent to well-meant assurances that time will heal the ache, our emotions strenuously deny any such possibility. We tend to search for some immediate escape route.

"Some people run away from grief, go on world cruises, or move to another town. But they do not escape, I think. The memories unbidden spring into their minds, scattered perhaps over the years. There is something to be said for facing them all deliberately and straightaway." So writes Sheldon Vanauken in *A Severe Mercy*.

As one who has twice suffered the trauma of parting with a dearly-loved wife, I can say from my own experience that while time does not and cannot remove the deep sense of loss, it does blunt the sharp edge of sorrow.

At times a sense of desolation will sweep over you, but these onslaughts diminish in frequency with the passage of time. If then with firm purpose we turn our thoughts away from ourselves toward meeting the needs of others, it is remarkable how our own grief is quieted.

There is a limited sense in which time is the great healer and consoler, but it is God, our loving Father, who holds that office, for He is "the Father of compassion and the God of all comfort, who comforts us in all our troubles" (2 Cor. 1:3–4). We should never lose sight of the fact that in the desert of our sorrow, there is the refreshing well of the comfort of God.

It was predicted of the coming Messiah that the Lord would send Him

> . . . *to bind up the brokenhearted,* . . . *to comfort all who mourn, and provide for those who grieve* in Zion—to bestow on them a crown of beauty instead of ashes, the oil of gladness instead of mourning, and a garment of praise instead of a spirit of despair (Is. 61:1–3; *italics mine*).

We must never underestimate what God can do for us in these circumstances, even though at the time the thought of receiving comfort seems a very remote possibility. He is "able to do immeasurably more than all we ask or imagine" (Eph. 3:20).

In his classic work *David Copperfield,* Charles Dickens depicts Mrs. Gummidge as the most utterly selfish and bad-tempered woman in Yarmouth. But when the town was caught up in a great disaster, she forgot herself in ministering to her needy neighbors in their distress. The experience transformed her. Copperfield was astounded at the unbelievable transformation in her character. Far from being self-centered, she now became a self-forgetful servant of the community. Dickens was a very discerning psychologist. Loneliness and self-forgetfulness cannot sleep in the same bed.

CHRISTIANS SORROW, BUT NOT AS OTHERS DO

It is possible for us to become so obsessed with our loss that we become overwhelmed with grief. While expressing our grief openly is beneficial and necessary, there can be an excess of grief that is damaging both psychologically and spiritually. And more important, it is dishonoring to our loving, caring, heavenly Father. It is right for Christians to sorrow as other men and women do, for being Christians does not dehumanize us. But we should not sorrow in the same way as those who have no hope beyond the grave.

The attitude of a Christian to the death of a loved one must seem paradoxical to those who have no personal experience of the love and care of our Father in heaven, those who do not share the hope He gives of a joyous reunion beyond the grave.

To most non-Christians, death is an unmitigated tragedy to be postponed for as long as possible. In the death of a believer there is a marked difference. The sorrow of those left behind is no less real and painful, but there are compensating factors that God brings into play, factors that stir up hope through the tears and shed light amid the gloom.

How can we who care for the departed loved one keep on grieving that our beloved has been released from the confinement of an ailing body and is now in the immediate presence of Christ, which Paul assures us is "far better"? To enjoy unending union with Him and revel in the communion of the saints is no cause for sorrow.

While not a certain cure for sorrow, concentration on these positive aspects surrounding the loss of a loved one will in some measure help to counteract an excessive dwelling upon our own sense of loss.

Hugging our sorrow and fueling our grief will only perpetuate the pain and render it even more difficult for us to recapture a semblance of normal life and usefulness in the community. We should not try to keep our grief alive, as do some who disbelieve that life can again return to near normalcy. To succumb to the negative view of things will make us the prisoner of our sorrow and prevent us from reaching out to fresh and stimulating goals in the days ahead.

Brothers, we do not want you to be ignorant about those who fall asleep, *or to grieve like the rest of men, who have no hope.* We believe that Jesus died and rose again and so we believe that God will bring with Jesus those who have fallen asleep in him (1 Thess. 4:13–14; *italics mine*).

Bishop Frank Houghton, my predecessor as General Director of Overseas Missionary Fellowship, displayed a mature attitude at the death of his younger sister, to whom he was very attached. In writing to his friend Amy Carmichael, founder of the Dohnavur Fellowship in India, he said:

Many of our friends in their letters of sympathy speak of God's mysterious ways, and I know there is an element of mystery. But I shrink from the suggestion that our Father has done anything that needs to be explained. What He has done is the best, because He has done it, and I pray that as a family we may not cast about for explanation, but exult in the Holy Spirit and say, "I thank thee, Father .... Even so Father ...." It suggests a lack of confidence in Him if we find it necessary to understand all that He does. Will it not bring greater joy to tell Him that we need no explanation because we know Him? "As for God, His way is perfect," said the psalmist. If His way is perfect we need no explanation.

We may not see just here and now
With vision clear the why and how

Of all that God seems to allow,
But "afterward" . . . .

FROM SORROW TO SERVICE

Josephine Butler, a noted British social worker, proved in a dramatic manner that a way to relieve one's own burden of sorrow is to shoulder that of someone else.

On coming home one day, her little daughter ran out of an upstairs room to greet her. She leaned over the balustrade to see her mother, but lost her balance, crashed to the ground, and died. The mother was broken-hearted, but the God of all comfort did not fail her in her distress.

An older Quaker lady came to comfort her and said, "I have spent most of my life looking after girls from the streets. I am old now and I can no longer handle the work of looking after the home where forty of them live. Come and take my job, and you will forget your sorrow."

Josephine took over the care of the home and found great fulfillment in doing so. While, of course, she never really forgot her sorrow, by taking on her shoulders the troubles and cares of others, she discovered a remedy for her own loss.

> Seldom can a heart be lonely
> If it seeks a lonelier still,
> Self-forgetful, longing only
> Emptier cups to fill.
> —Eleanor Standinmeyer

GOD CARES FOR THE WIDOWED

In loving, you and I assume the risk of loss. . . .
We're so happy now, but we must accept the
fact that one of us will have to live without
the other some day.
—Helen Raley, On Being a Widow

From whatever point of view it is approached, the lot of the widow—or widower—is anything but enviable. Theirs is essentially a lonely sorrow that in most cases is not easily overcome.

All married couples, if they are realists, must sooner or later face the fact that in the course of time one of them will walk the remaining pathway of life alone. Statistics tell us that the wife is much more likely to survive. Increasingly, the life expectancy of women continues to outpace that of men. It is not morbid to face this indisputable reality. Rather it is wise to do so, for too many spouses have to meet the dreaded crisis unprepared.

In her book *Alone*, Katie F. Wiebe tells of one recently bereaved wife whose husband had been ill for a long time. The woman recounted her reaction when at last he was taken from her:

Though I had lived with Walter's illness for several years, steeling myself for the eventuality of his death, I found myself as unprepared as a passenger in a boat who is suddenly dumped into the water. I realize now that this state of blank bewilderment is fairly normal for anyone moving through the grief process.

Perhaps some starkly realistic forethought and planning might have greatly reduced the trauma of the experience and its inevitable side effects.

But no matter how carefully we may have conditioned ourselves for the possible passing of our partner, or how realistically we may have prepared ourselves in mind for the actual transition, inevitably there comes the shock and the grim reality of the final parting. Its effects can be overwhelming. Not infrequently, for a time it saps the very will to live through the bleakness of the widowed state.

When we are in the early stages of grief, some well-meaning friend will assure us that time is a great healer. But in the throes of despair it seems only another empty cliché, utterly removed from reality. It may be true in the case of others, but it could not be in our case.

The dark reality that cannot be evaded is that the loved one is no longer there to love and be loved. A companionship that has grown dearer and deeper with the years is not readily replaced, nor is the aching void speedily filled.

It was Søren Kierkegaard's contention that suffering is inexpressible. There is also a very real sense in which the suffering and loneliness of the widowed, too, cannot be expressed and must be borne alone.

There is a mystery of human hearts,
And though encircled by a host
Of those who love us well, and are beloved,
To every one of us from time to time
There comes a sense of utter loneliness.

Our dearest friend is stranger to our joy,
And cannot realize our bitterness.
"There is not one who really understands,
No one to enter in to what I feel."
Such is the cry of each of us in turn.

We wander in a solitary way,
No matter what our lot may be;
Each heart, mysterious even to itself,
Must live its inner life in solitude.

These poignant lines portray the experience of most of us. But for the Christian, while the sense of loss is no less real, there is a compensating factor that is not mentioned in the poem—the comforting presence of the God of all comfort.

Praise be to the God and Father of our Lord
Jesus Christ, the Father of compassion and
the God of all comfort, who comforts us in all
our troubles, so that we can comfort those in
any trouble with the comfort we ourselves
have received from God (2 Cor. 1:3–4).

Speaking from experience, I know that in the early days of bereavement, widows and widowers receive a great deal of sympathy and support from relatives and friends who are genuinely concerned to alleviate in some measure the grief of those they love. They receive many invitations out to meals and other social occasions. Friends drop in for a chat now and again. But amid the hectic pressures of our age, the demands of life are so great that almost inevitably the number of visitors declines and invitations out become fewer. It is not that our friends have ceased caring, but there is a limit to what can be crowded into one day.

THE BIBLICAL OUTLOOK

In our western society there is a tendency, not always conscious or intentional, to neglect or even ostracize widows. This was not the case in Old Testament times. God ordained that special provision be made for them, and He expressed His concern lest they be exploited.

> Do not take advantage of a widow or an orphan. If you do and they cry out to me, I will certainly hear their cry. My anger will be aroused (Ex. 22:22–24).

When instructing the Israelites concerning their behavior upon entering into their inheritance in Canaan, God, through Moses, gave further expression of His concern:

> Do not . . . take the cloak of a widow as a

pledge. . . . When you are harvesting in
your field and you overlook a sheaf, do not
go back to get it. Leave it for the alien, the
fatherless and the widow (Deut. 24:17, 19).

A similar charitable attitude was to be observed
when they were harvesting grapes and olives. The
charming biblical story of Ruth illustrates the manner in which this instruction was carried out by the
caring Israelite.

The New Testament is no less eager to protect
the widow. Acts 6:1–3 shows how the apostles
viewed and handled this situation in the earliest
days of the church. The Hellenistic Jews lodged a
complaint with the apostles that their widows were
being overlooked in the daily distribution of food.
The apostles immediately demonstrated their concern that the widows should receive equitable treatment. Seven men of ability and integrity were
selected by the church to oversee this worthy social
service.

Both Paul and James challenged the churches
to which they wrote to act responsibly towards the
widows among them (1 Tim. 5:3–16; James 1:27).

The psalmist had a true conception of the God
of the widow when he wrote: "A father to the fatherless, a defender of the widows, is God in his holy
dwelling" (Ps. 68:5).

PRACTICAL PROBLEMS

When the husband has been the popular mate and
the life of the party, loneliness can become even
more acute. A friend recently told me about his

daughter and her husband who moved to another city. They purchased a home in a new suburb where few of the houses were completed. Consequently there were few neighbors, and they had not been sufficiently long in the community to establish close relationships.

When, as the result of an accident, her husband was killed, the widow was left alone with two little children. Most of the acquaintances they had made were friends of the husband rather than companions of her own making. Suddenly she found herself bereaved; living in a sparsely inhabited neighborhood, in a strange city with few friends; all alone with her grief; and facing a desolate future. In our great cities similar tragic situations can be multiplied a hundredfold.

It is sometimes assumed or suggested that the lot of the widower is less distressing than that of the widow. This is doubtless true in many cases, but in our contemporary society, though the plight of the widower is no less acute, it attracts much less concern.

In the anguish of his unexpected bereavement, C. S. Lewis penned these words in *A Grief Observed*: "Oh God, why did you take so much trouble to force this creature out of its shell, if it is now doomed to crawl back—to be sucked back—into it?"

A widower is frequently less equipped to handle the changed circumstances than is his feminine counterpart. This is especially so if he is not familiar with household duties. The situation becomes even more complicated and stressful when children are left in his care. He feels at a desperate disadvantage, and life can become a harrowing experience when this responsibility is added to the burden of his grief.

Perhaps out of his own experience Alfred Lord Tennyson wrote:

> Tears of a widower when he sees
> A late lost form that sleep reveals,
> And moves his doubtful arms and feels
> Her place is empty—fall like these.

My second wife, now with the Lord, had been a widow for many years. She had felt the loneliness of widowhood very keenly. If she went out in the evening to attend a meeting or social function, she found returning to the lonely house a daunting and desolating experience, the poignancy of which did not fade with the passing years.

Lord Byron knew something of the same emotion:

> 'Tis sweet to hear the watchdog's bark
> Bay deep-mouthed welcome as we draw
> near home;
> 'Tis sweet to know there is an eye will mark
> Our coming, and will look brighter when
> we come.

In writing of her reactions after her husband's death, Helen Raley made this observation in her book, *On Being a Widow*:

> I was to learn that although widowhood presents a woman sometimes as a non-person or a half-person, she need not suc-

cumb to the hopeless abandonment of life. Nor need she forget, for any reason, the identity she once shared with her husband. Awareness of this is a way towards selfhood, a disciplined motivation and a measure of contentment. . . . For the survivor, life must go on. The death of a loved one does not mean the end of all things, and somehow, sooner or later, reality must be faced.

In his book *Kathleen,* written shortly after his own bereavement, Edward Blaiklock, my friend of sixty years, recorded this prayer, which is especially appropriate for the widowed:

Father, we pray for all lonely people, especially for those who, coming home to an empty house, stand at the door hesitant, afraid to enter. May all who stand in a doorway with fear in their hearts, like the two on the Emmaus road, ask the Living One in. Then, by His grace, may they find that in loneliness they are never alone, and that He peoples empty rooms with His presence.

THE LONELINESS OF DIVORCE

No one gets out completely unscarred. When people
who have grown together are separated, it's never a
simple, clean disconnection. It's like pulling a tree
out of the ground—it's a violent act, and you can't do
it without some damage.
—Tim Stafford, "Love, Sex, and the Whole Person"

While divorce may provide a solution for some marriage problems, it usually creates more complexities than it solves. Many people who have experienced it contend that divorce can introduce one of the most desolate periods of life.

In the midst of the emotional turmoil that precipitates divorce, couples pay insufficient attention to the far-reaching side consequences that will accrue. Only after the final break has taken place is the shattering discovery made that totally unexpected side-effects are involved. The parties failed to face the implications realistically before the irrevocable step was taken.

The soaring divorce rate around the world, an unhappy distinctive of our times, is creating an increasing community of the lonely. Especially in the affluent developed countries, with their plummeting moral standards, divorce has escalated at such a pace as to seriously threaten the very institution of marriage.

In my youth I did not know one divorced Christian. The case is far different today. In Britain, on present trends, one marriage in three will end in divorce. In the United States there is one divorce for every 1.8 marriages. (Happily, the latest figures indicate a slight decrease in the rate of divorce.) From 1960 to 1980 the number of divorced men and women more than tripled. This means that divorce has now reached epidemic proportions and one serious consequence is, according to past experience, that what happens in America today will happen in other countries tomorrow. In Britain experts estimate that one child in five will experience the divorce of their parents before reaching the age of sixteen.

One survey revealed that only one third of American homes are made up of both parents and their children. Single-parent families are increasing twenty times as fast as two-parent families. Real estate agents report that a great deal of the movement in the property market is a spin-off of this phenomenal rise in broken homes.

THE PLIGHT OF CHILDREN
One can hardly bear thinking about the toll of emotional distress and insecurity that this tragic development exacts from the children involved in these separations and divorces. Every lonely, unhappy person inevitably creates and diffuses an atmo-

sphere of emotional tension and silent misery that soon spreads to others.

There is little doubt that the innocent children who are the victims of these fractured marriages suffer more severely than their parents because they feel the consequent loss of love and security more severely than do mature adults. They become confused because often they do not know to whom to turn for emotional help and support.

The resulting insecurity of this group spills over into their own subsequent marriage relationships. It is not surprising that many feel that since their parents' marriage ended in divorce, they cannot feel secure in their own union. Divorce thus becomes a self-perpetuating agony. Much of the subsequent marriage break up within this group can be traced back to the trauma caused by the divorce of their own parents.

Few children emerge from these family situations without deep emotional scars. A report in the *Journal of the Royal College of General Practitioners* showed that preschool children were confused and frightened and blamed themselves for the break up. They expressed fears of being sent away from home.

The divorce of parents caused more problems when it occurred before the children were five than when it happened later. School children expressed feelings of sadness and rejection, but did not blame themselves. Children over the age of nine more often expressed anger and outrage at their parents' behavior; they felt lonely and rejected. Teenagers also expressed these feelings and felt shame and embarrassment. By young adulthood there was a higher incidence of illegitimate births, divorce, stomach ulcers, and emotional problems among children of divorced parents.

In many cases, it was the children and their future custody after the divorce that lay at the heart of the quarreling, and this tends to generate in the children an unwarranted sense of guilt. They feel that in some way they are to blame for the rupture.

One psychologist maintains that the trauma of divorce is second only to the death of a loved one, and this is especially the case with children. When the familiar family structure collapses, the child is bewildered and feels lonely and frightened.

The children affected have to face many perplexing situations at an age when they are ill-equipped to cope with them. The question of loyalty arises. To which parent? They are pulled in both directions. They face the loss of one of their parents, and as often happens, they may also be separated from school and church friends through removal to another area. This can make very deep wounds that carry over into the future relationships.

When parents are contemplating the possibility of divorce, in their preoccupation with the problems of their own relationships, they do not always face sympathetically the consequences to the children of the marriage.

To incorporate a new father or mother into the family structure is never an easy transition, and more often than not it produces adverse reactions on the part of the children.

DIVORCE LEADS TO
CHRONIC LONELINESS

Both research and experience combine to predict that divorce is more likely to lead to chronic loneliness than even the loss of a loved one, and this is for several reasons:

- Both parents involved usually emerge from the crisis with feelings of guilt, failure, and depression, all of which provide fuel for loneliness.
- The parent to whom custody of the children is entrusted, in an understandable desire to secure or retain their affection, will be under strong temptation to denigrate the estranged partner to the children.
- The divorce may result in the total rejection of one spouse by the children, or—in the unhappy situation where different children favor different parents—they too may become divided among themselves.
- If the divorced parent entertains friends in the home, the children are likely to feel in the way and unwanted.
- Divorce usually springs from and generates unresolved conflict, which leaves scars on every member of the family unit. These may take a long time to heal.

Factors producing loneliness as a result of divorce are many. Although the marriage partnership may have been less than ideal, at least it provided a semblance of companionship for both partners. At least the home was not empty. There was someone there with whom to share, even though it might be superficially, the joys and trials of daily life; someone with whom to consult when decisions must be made; someone to converse with at mealtimes.

The absence of these contacts creates an even more unsatisfactory situation. But too often this discovery is made only after the fatal step is taken. Then, too, the signing of the decree does not always take away the desire for physical intimacy. A comfortable adjustment to the changed lifestyle is not achieved immediately. Coming home to a cold and empty house is no experience to be coveted.

UNWELCOME SIDE-EFFECTS

One of the unexpected and unwelcome results of divorce is that often friends begin to drop off, especially if they are friends of the estranged spouse. They feel that they have to take sides. Invitations to social occasions come less frequently because in our couples-orientated society a divorcee is sometimes regarded as a sexual threat.

An even more painful possibility may surface— the alienation of members of one's own family, with a consequent loss of love and support at the time when it is most needed.

The tragic factor is that a relationship that began with such high expectations, and in an atmosphere of love, has died. And now there is the legal process with all it involves—the division of assets and other necessary but heartbreaking decisions. It has been likened to an amputation. The pain is not over when the legal process has been finalized.

A sense of failure in not having been able to make the marriage work, or in not successfully fulfilling the role of a parent, does nothing to heal the hurt or calm the loneliness.

To Christian divorcees, one of the most painful aspects of divorce emerges when they find that sometimes even fellow church members, friends of long standing, are cool and embarrassed in their company. Divorce always opens the door to possible misunderstanding, and even to unloving attitudes.

It must be emphasized, and strongly, that one essential element in alleviating the loneliness of divorce is for the estranged partners to genuinely forgive from the heart, no matter how they each may have been at fault. An unforgiving spirit acts as a cancer in the soul.

Our Lord left no doubt about the necessity of forgiving those whom we feel have sinned against us.

And when you stand praying, if you hold anything against anyone, *forgive him,* so that your Father in heaven may forgive you your sins (Mark 11:25; *italics mine*).

Forgive us our debts, *as we also have forgiven* our debtors (Matt. 6:12; *italics mine*).

10

THE LONELY UNEMPLOYED

As one of the unemployed, may I suggest that
what we look for in our crisis is a spirit of
discernment from those who come in touch with
us. We don't want sympathy. Unemployment is a
very personal and private thing. Don't try to
understand it, or stand in judgment . . . . After all,
unemployment is a traumatic and a tender time for
those who are its victims.
—Michael Holmes

The relentless onward march of electronics, automation, nuclear technology, and computers is leaving in its wake an ever-increasing company of the unemployed. A whole generation of young men and women, with all their unrealized potential, faces the grim prospect of going through life without ever obtaining a job.

An older generation, still willing and capable of doing valuable work, find themselves put out to pasture, redundant. And the tragedy of their situation is that the prognosis for their ever gaining employment is bleak indeed. The physical and psychological effects of this situation are a matter of deep concern. The loneliness of the unemployed is one of the distressing maladies of our era for which no cure has yet been found by politicians or business tycoons.

Until unemployment enters the arena of our own circle or personal experience, we are inclined to regard it as something regrettable but inevitable—a remote and unpleasant accompaniment of the march of progress. But when it invades our own circle and strikes us or our loved ones, the reality can be devastating.

Michael Holmes, a New Zealand journalist and public consultant, gave an interview, which was published in a local newspaper, in which he frankly opened his heart and spoke for many of his fellow-sufferers. It was his desire to help those in a similar plight. I quote it at length, so that readers may gain a more realistic and compassionate view of what victims of this worldwide social ill have to contend with, and of the corrosive loneliness that results.

He talks freely of the manner in which unemployment affected him and his family. His case will be fairly typical of a large segment of unemployed people, except that he had the inner resource that comes through being a practicing Christian. This proved to be the determining factor in his ability to survive the testing times.

He had attained a fairly comfortable position in life, and the possibility of becoming unemployed had never entered his thoughts. Thus it was something akin to an earthquake when he first became unemployed. The trauma continued for a total of fourteen months, as he went through three prolonged periods of unemployment. He tells his story:

I had always been a confident, self-assured person, but suddenly all that was stripped away and the reality and horror of unemployment had me in its grip. It seemed that I had missed the bus and was now a victim of society's work scrap-heap. I felt devastated and thought the world had left me behind.

True, I had made some errors of judgment, but I never thought I would drop to such a low level of despair. My self-esteem crashed, and I felt worthless to myself, my family, my friends, the church, and even God Himself.

The impression of rejection only consolidated as my position became clear, and hopelessness settled on me. I did not want to face people and found myself withdrawing into myself. I began to lose my self-confidence, and as the opportunity for work diminished with each job application, I found myself panicking as to whether I would ever get a meaningful job again.

Bills still had to be met, teenage mouths fed, and the family still had to be motivated. Boredom is an emotional and spiritual killer, and time lay heavily on my hands as I waited anxiously for some response to many applications.

The stigma of being unemployed is very real. To the employed and unemployed alike, unemployment is a social embarrassment. People are often nonplused as to how to react and often withdraw. Government agencies tend to treat you as less than a real person, and even prospective employers look at you with a jaundiced eye.

Initially the full impact of what had happened was not too bad. There was an air of optimism that all would be well in a week or two. However, as the weeks rolled into months, the clouds began to get darker.

As the situation went from bad to worse (I applied for more than 100 positions earlier this year before I obtained my present temporary one), I began to realize that as a Christian, I could no longer look to man for my solutions, but only God was my ultimate deep emotional and spiritual anchor.

Job's comforters were two-a-penny. Barriers went up. Well-meaning people, ignorant of what it is like to be unemployed and without too much thought for finer feelings, said things which made us feel hurt and distrustful. Having people say, "We think you should try such and such," or, "We think you are not doing enough about getting work," was frustrating.

In a sense you got the feeling they were self-appointed "guardians" of the social security system, watching how we used the dole and how we lived. Often I gained the impression I and my family were an object of curiosity.

Applying for a job when you are in your forties is almost an impossible task. I tried for all types of jobs, from Post Office commissionaire to chauffeur, and to more exotic positions. One of the biggest frustrations was applying for a job which wanted a mature and experienced person, only to find they wanted someone not over twenty-five!

Unemployment is a draining time, emotionally, physically, and spiritually. But through it all we found our local church most supportive, and encouraging and practical. Well, you may ask, "Where is God through all this?" Like the psalmist I often asked myself why I was cast down, and always His answer came back, "Hope thou in God." My faith, background, life experiences and Bible training and my church ministry enabled the Holy Spirit to bring many things to my remembrance.

Patience is another ingredient. Even though I was desperate, I am glad that God stopped me from getting certain jobs, proving the truth of Galatians 4:4, "In the fullness of time, God . . . ." I have learned also that when you are in a position of comfort and affluence, it is so easy to speak glibly about trusting God.

When you are down in the depths of despair, when faith is being put to the test, to be able to say, "I know whom I have believed and am persuaded that he is able to keep that which I have committed . . . ." is a far more lasting and real truth.

That's what God is all about. He is real when you are down. I have been there and know that God is able to do exceeding abundantly above all that I or my family could ever ask or think.

As one of the unemployed, may I suggest that what we look for in our crisis is a spirit of discernment from those who come in touch with us. We don't want sympathy. Unemployment is a very personal and private thing. Don't try to understand it, or stand in judgment . . . . After all, unemployment is a traumatic and a tender time for those who are its victims.

This starkly honest account of the agonizing experience many of our contemporaries are passing through, while bypassing none of the desolation of the experience, shows how the Christian, through faith in God and the support of fellow Christians, is enabled to triumph in the midst of tragedy.

11

THE LONELINESS OF LEADERSHIP

On without cheer of brother or of daughter,
Yes, without stay of father or of son,
Lone on the land, and homeless on the water,
Pass I in patience till my work be done.
—F. W. H. Myers, "St. Paul"

In his matchless poem, "St. Paul," F. W. H. Myers puts these luminous words into the mouth of the apostle. They certainly speak eloquently to his own situation as he traversed land and sea with the Good News. It was A. W. Tozer who said that most of the world's great souls have been lonely. That seems to be part of the price saints must pay for their saintliness. And it would be equally true that it is usually part of the price of responsible leadership.

When Paul was confined in a Roman prison awaiting his impending martyrdom, it was a very human touch that he should beg his son in the faith, Timothy, to come to him before winter because he was so lonely (2 Tim. 4:9–21). Being a saint and a leader had not lifted him above the need of congenial human companionship.

No one who has shouldered the burden of

responsible leadership will find difficulty in identifying with Moses when he complained to God saying, "I cannot carry all these people by myself; the burden is too heavy for me" (Num. 11:14).

In every leadership position, crises will arise sooner or later, when the burden of responsibility seems far beyond one's ability to bear it. Paul found himself in such a position when ministering in the province of Asia.

> *We were under great pressure, far beyond our ability to endure,* so that we despaired even of life. Indeed, in our hearts we felt the sentence of death. But this happened that we might not rely on ourselves but on God, who raises the dead (2 Cor. 1:8–9; *italics mine*).

But the God in whom he trusted carried him through.

From its very nature the role of a leader must be a rather lonely one, for they must always be ahead of their followers in some areas. Though they be the most friendly and gregarious of people, inevitably there will be some paths they must be prepared to tread alone. It was Nietzsche's contention that life always gets harder near the summit—the cold increases and the path becomes more difficult. Mountain climbers affirm the truth that "the higher you go, the lonelier it gets."

This fact dawned dramatically on Dixon E. Hoste, one of the famous missionary "Cambridge Seven," when Hudson Taylor, founder of the China

Inland Mission, passed the reins of leadership into his hands. The China Inland Mission was the first of the so-called "Faith Missions," and it was at that time the largest.

After the momentous interview during which the frail leader passed on the torch to his successor, Hoste, deeply moved and sensible of the weight of responsibility that now rested on his shoulders, said to himself, "And now I have no one but God." Alone, yet not alone.

THE PRICE OF LEADERSHIP

Human nature craves companionship and it is a natural desire for a leader to wish to share with others the burdens of care, especially when decisions of far-reaching consequence must be made. It is heartbreaking at times for a leader to have to make adverse decisions affecting the future of loved colleagues—and make them alone. This is one of the costliest aspects of leadership, but sometimes it must be paid if one's leadership is to be productive.

Moses paid a steep price for his leadership—alone on the mount, and then alone on the plain. When his father-in-law, Jethro, came to pay his daughter and grandchildren a visit, he was appalled at the emotional and spiritual expenditure Moses' leadership was exacting. He tendered very sound advice, which Moses was wise enough to accept—advice that is equally fitting for today's overburdened Christian leaders and executives who find themselves thrust into stressful situations.

[Jethro] replied, "What you are doing is not

good. You and these people who come to you will only wear yourselves out. The work is too heavy for you; you cannot handle it alone. . . . But select capable men from all the people . . . and appoint them as officials. . . . Have them serve as judges for the people at all times, but have them bring every difficult case to you" (Ex. 18:17–18, 21–22).

Moses found the answer to the isolation and loneliness of his leadership in the wise delegation and sharing of responsibility. His loneliness was more than the situation demanded and only served to make him unfit for his work. Those in leadership positions are often slow to master this important lesson and pay the price in impaired health.

THE LONELINESS OF MISJUDGMENT

Moses experienced another painful type of loneliness—the crushing load of unjustified or jealous criticism and misunderstanding.

Miriam and Aaron began to talk against Moses because of his Cushite wife, for he had married a Cushite. "Has the Lord spoken only through Moses?" they asked. "Hasn't he also spoken through us?" (Num. 12:1–2).

Though totally unselfish and disinterested in his service for the nation, his motivation was impugned. The fact that some of the criticism came from his own sister and brother rendered it even more hurtful.

Tom Bracken revealed keen insight into the nature of this kind of trial when he wrote:

Not understood! We move along asunder;
Our paths grow wider as the seasons creep
Along the years; we marvel and we wonder
Why life is life, and then we fall asleep,
Not understood.

Not understood! How many breasts are aching
For lack of sympathy. Ah, day by day
How many cheerless, lonely hearts are breaking,
How many noble spirits pass away
Not understood.

O God! That men would see a little clearer,
Or judge less harshly when they cannot see!
O God! That men would draw a littler nearer
To one another—they'd be nearer Thee—
And understood!

THE LONELY PROPHET

The prophets of Israel were lonely men. In the dawn of history the prophet Enoch walked alone in a decadent society because his consistent walk with God necessarily led him in the opposite direction to that traveled by his ungodly contemporaries (Jude 14–15).

Who experienced the pangs of loneliness more deeply than the prophet Jonah as he trod the lonely streets of pagan Nineveh? It was to a city of a million inhabitants that he announced the unwelcome message of impending judgment: "Forty more days and Nineveh will be overturned" (3:4).

John the Baptist, the last and probably the loneliest of the long line of prophets, lived a great deal of his life in the solitude of the desert. His austere lifestyle and uncompromising message condemned him to a solitary life. And yet it was he who received from the Master a eulogy accorded to no other: "I tell you the truth: Among those born of women there has not risen anyone greater than John the Baptist" (Matt. 11:11).

John did not permit his loneliness to deter him from exercising a mighty ministry. Does this have something to say to us?

Today the loneliest preacher is probably the one to whom God has entrusted a prophetic message that cuts right across the prevailing temper of the age. The preacher who is ahead of his times is doomed to plow a lonely furrow.

The gregarious Paul often experienced the pangs of loneliness and bitterness of being misjudged and misunderstood by his contemporaries. More bitter still, he was misconstrued even by some of his own children in the faith. Few things are more hurtful to a leader than the defection or desertion of friends or converts. What pathos Paul packs into these words: "You know that everyone in the province of Asia has deserted me" (2 Tim. 1:15). Unfortunately, in our own day similar situations occur all too frequently.

In his book *The Team Concept,* Bruce Stabbert evaluates the advantage of a team ministry over against the one-man ministry with its built in loneliness. He writes:

There is an isolation and loneliness to the one-pastor ministry that is largely unnecessary. With a team there is a sharing of burdens in brotherly comity. Many pastors say that the ministry is lonely, but unavoidably so. Frequently a single pastor has no one in whom he can confide his frustrations, struggles and disappointments, with the exception of his wife. He may have no one to stand alongside him when he is too readily admonished by self-appointed critics.

The words of the wise man are singularly appropriate in such a situation:

Two are better than one, because they have a good return for their work: If one falls down, his friend can help him up. But pity the man who falls and has no one to help him up! Also, if two lie down together, they will keep warm. But how can one keep warm alone? (Eccl. 4:9–11).

THREE CONTRIBUTORY ELEMENTS

To you, O Lord, I lift up my soul; in you I trust, O
my God.... Turn to me and be gracious to me, for I
am lonely and afflicted.... my hope is in you.
—Psalm 25:1, 16, 21

THE LONELINESS OF TEMPERAMENT

The temperament with which one is endowed without doubt plays a significant part in determining the degree of one's vulnerability to the inroads of loneliness. Those blessed with a sanguine temperament with its optimistic window on life in general should be less liable to fall prey to it than those whose temperament tends towards the melancholic.

In the melancholic person, feeling is a much more potent factor than it is with the sanguine. The former tends to be more introspective and withdrawn. He spends a good deal of time photographing his emotional states and developing the films.

This chronic inward-looking and often negative self-appraisal makes him self-absorbed, and thus a prime target for loneliness. However, that condition is not confined to the melancholic, for it can be experienced in differing degrees by every major personality type, given the conducive circumstances.

Of course none of us is responsible for the temperament we have inherited, whether it be sanguine, melancholic, or some other combination of types. But we are responsible for the way in which we react and control it. We are not caught helplessly in the grip of necessity, and we need not remain its slaves. But unless we are alert and watchful of its tendency, we could easily become the plaything of our temperament. On the other hand, we must guard against the danger of regarding as spiritual failure what may be only an involuntary temperamental reaction in which there is no guilt.

In treating this aspect of the problem, Arthur Pierson, in his work *Godly Self-Control,* suggested that we should be careful to

> . . . distinguish between what is temperamental and what is properly spiritual in our human experience. In dealing with people, the sagacious counselor will always draw a clear line of discrimination between what is impulsive and involuntary and what is deliberate and voluntary. Only the latter rightly belongs to the deeper spiritual life.
>
> There are traits inherited from immediate or remote ancestors that are no more a matter of personal choice than the color of our hair or eyes, and therefore are destitute of proper moral quality.

We are not responsible for the capricious and

involuntary undulations of our emotions—only for the definite choices of our will. We are what we choose, not what we feel. If we grasp this distinction, it could deliver us from the pain of much false guilt.

In referring to the built-in tendency of the melancholic to indulge in morbid introspection, Professor O. Hallesby of Norway had this to say in his book *Temperament in the Christian Life:*

His introspection, however, may lead him to religious brooding. He has a tendency to devote himself to the more difficult passages of Scripture. These can turn him away from the Bible's simple statements about sin and grace, and thus weaken his spiritual life.

This adds up to the fact that the person of a predominantly melancholic turn of mind is more vulnerable to the experience of loneliness than any of the other temperaments. But though he may give the impression of being distant and withdrawn, behind the sometimes forbidding exterior there beats a warm heart. The likelihood is that he has a secret longing for close companionship but does not know how to go about it.

At the other extreme are those who in their desperate attempts to relieve their loneliness may make such excessive demands on the time and affections of others that they actually defeat their own desire. Being overpossessive, or jealous and exclusive in a friendship should be diligently avoided if there is to be an easy and mutually-enjoyable relationship.

Loneliness begets a negative frame of mind in which it is easier to see the darker side of life than the bright. The optimist sees the bottle half full. The pessimist sees the same bottle half empty. The same attitude persists in the depressed and lonely person's approach to Scripture. He finds it much easier to identify with the condemning passages than with those that breathe assurance and confidence. But if we come to Scripture in that frame of mind, we will be likely to find what we expect.

A young woman who had doubts about the factuality of Christ's bodily resurrection was asked to lead a study group at an Easter camp, and she was naturally in a quandary. How could she teach what she had doubts about herself? She consulted Miss Ruth Paxson, a well-known Bible teacher, and asked her to go through the resurrection passage in Matthew 28 with her. They came to verse 17: "When they saw him, they worshiped him; *but some doubted*" (italics mine). "How could they help doubting?" the girl said. "Now isn't that strange," replied Miss Paxson. "When I read that verse, my thought was, How could they help worshiping?"

THE LONELINESS OF REJECTION

One common factor that contributes to loneliness is the experience of rejection, or the fear of being rejected. It is a condition most of us face in some areas of life.

Once a person's friendly advances have met with coldness or rebuff, and especially so if he or she is shy and sensitive, it becomes increasingly difficult to summon up the courage to risk another rejection.

Instead, the tendency will be to retreat further into oneself in an effort to avoid being hurt again.

Members of other ethnic groups who emigrate to our western lands all too often meet with a cool reception. Instead of receiving a warm welcome to their adopted homeland, they are ignored or rejected. In many cases they had escaped from their own disturbed country with high hopes of a new and better life opening out before them; but those hopes have been realized only partially and they have found themselves not fully accepted, lonely in a strange land. Immigrant workers who for periods leave their impoverished homelands to earn a precarious living to help support relatives they have left behind meet with a very cold reception. Of course there are glorious exceptions, but the attitude outlined is far too common.

The indifference or at times exploitation that these newcomers experience in the host country breeds a basic distrust of those who employ them or with whom they work. Having been rebuffed or ignored so often, they become hesitant to make further advances and instead retreat into their lonely ghettos.

A somewhat kindred attitude develops in some aging people who feel—by no means always with just cause—that they are no longer needed or wanted by anyone. "Of what use am I to anyone?" they moan. "I am just cluttering up the ground" is the agonized cry of some neglected and rejected souls.

If they meet with further rejection, their understandable reaction is to doubt their self-worth even more. Feeling that they are merely tolerated, not welcomed, they shrink back into their own sad little world.

Paradoxically, it is among the younger generation that loneliness is most prevalent and its pain most acute. The fear of lack of acceptance among their peers, or even outright rejection, in many cases becomes almost pathological. Even though it may be masked by boisterous or outrageous behavior, the loneliness generated is intense, and we older people should be sensitive to this possibility and be reasonably tolerant in our attitude to them.

In *Understanding Loneliness*, by Edgar Jackson, the author tells how Margaret Mead, the noted anthropologist, went to De Pauw University filled with hope and excitement. She wanted to enter into campus life to the full, and in her mind this included the social life of a sorority. But her application for membership was declined. The wounds of that rejection cut deeply into the very core of her being. She survived the loss, but its effect was so great that later it made her very sensitive to the needs of excluded people. Doubtless that traumatic experience contributed greatly to her understanding of all peoples.

But not every freshman is sufficiently resilient to emerge unscarred from so painful an experience as that suffered by Margaret Mead. In some, rejection causes great and permanent psychological damage that handicaps them for life. This in turn causes them to reject the friendly advances of others.

Experience attests that it is the person who takes the rejection or rebuff in stride, rises and tries again, who will overcome the fundamental problem. The one who fails to do this and passively succumbs will in all probability lapse into even deeper isolation.

THE LONELINESS OF FAILURE

"Failure is one of the uglies of life," wrote Howard Hendricks. And who of us can claim that we have not experienced failure? Whether Christian or non-Christian, we have all failed in some areas of our lives. There has been only One who has never failed.

With some, the failure has involved gross and disreputable sin. With others it may have been more respectable and socially acceptable sins, such as pride, envy, gossip, and covetousness. But none will claim freedom from failure, except those who hold very superficial views of the sinfulness of sin.

An increasing number—Christian leaders and workers among them—are facing failure and breakdown in the marriage relationship or in the area of parenting. Such failure was present in past days, but today it is much more difficult to conceal. It has grown alarmingly common and is open to public view. At the time of this writing the failures of prominent Christian and political personalities are being flashed around the world, but evidence of regret and repentance on the part of some seems to be a missing element.

In many cases the failure is a lonely, personal secret, shared with no one else, but none the less distressing because of that. Loneliness is an inevitable accessory of failure because it is essentially personal. "It was I who perpetrated it." "I alone am responsible for it and the resulting consequences."

Failure, the fear of exposure, and fear of further

failure lead the one who has failed to a withdrawal from intimacy with others, lest they discover what he or she is really like. The victims thus become the prisoners of their own thoughts and guilt. So to preserve their reputation, they pursue the counterproductive course of retreating into themselves.

David followed this course, and as a result experienced the bitterness and loneliness of moral failure throughout that black year when he stubbornly refused to repent and confess his sin with Bathsheba. Hear his tragic confession:

> When I kept silent, my bones wasted away through my groaning all day long. For day and night your hand was heavy upon me; my strength was sapped as in the heat of summer. Then I acknowledged my sin to you and did not cover up my iniquity. I said, "I will confess my transgressions to the Lord"—and you forgave the guilt of my sin (Ps. 32:3–5).

David's heartbroken sobs as he made confession of his sin in Psalm 51 are an indication of his sense of isolation from God, which is the sure result of his unconfessed sin. The lesson for us is plain.

But note the shout of joy and release when, after his abject confession, he appropriated the divine forgiveness and burst out of the icehouse of his shame and loneliness: "Blessed is he whose transgressions are forgiven and whose sins are covered. Blessed is the man whose sin the Lord does not count against him" (Ps. 32:1–2).

114

13

THE DEVIL'S PECULIAR WORKSHOP

There are only two possible centers for life—God and self. If we are not becoming centered on God, we are becoming centered upon self; and self-centeredness is the essence of sin. The Jews—and we—may seek for the Light of the World, the Life of life, but so far as we remain self-centered, we can never find it.
—Archbishop William Temple

It was the Puritan saint William Law who described self as "the devil's peculiar workshop." If he is correct in his perception, then one of Satan's most effective tools in achieving his subtle objectives must be the scourge of loneliness.

THE SNARE OF SELF-PITY
"Indulging in self-pity is a one-way ticket to the experience of loneliness," says one counselor. The Christian who shifts the center of life from Christ to self thereby exposes himself to many spiritual maladies. Because self-pity tacitly denies personal responsibility for one's condition, there can be no successful strategy for conquering loneliness so long as that attitude is indulged and maintained.

Elijah the prophet is the classic biblical example of a true man of God who became engulfed in the morass of self-pity and loneliness. It was after his epic encounter with Ahab and Jezebel, in which God gave him a notable victory, that his fall came.

The story is replete with instruction and encouragement for any who may be in like case. The root cause of his condition was diagnosed by God Himself, and He it was who prescribed the remedy. Elijah's sorry plight is epitomized in these words:

> Elijah was afraid and ran for his life. When he came to Beersheba in Judah, he left his servant there, while he himself went a day's journey into the desert. He came to a broom tree and sat down under it and prayed that he might die. "I have had enough, Lord," he said. "Take my life; I am no better than my ancestors" (1 Kin. 19:3–4).

A more extreme example of depression, self-pity, and loneliness it would be difficult to conceive, and as it is so relevant to the subject of our study, a detailed consideration of its lessons is warranted.

The satanic shaft struck Elijah when it would least have been expected. Surely elation would have been a more appropriate response. Had he not inflicted a stunning defeat on King Ahab, and had he not won a spectacular victory over the pagan and Baal and his followers?

But there were hidden reasons for his depression and loneliness, as there doubtless are with ours. What was it that caused him to cry mistakenly in his acute loneliness, "I am the only one left, and now they are trying to kill me too" (1 Kin. 19:10)?

There was a physiological cause. One has only to reflect on the tremendous emotional and physical expenditure involved in his confrontation on Mount Carmel—one lone man against a whole nation sunk deep in idolatry, then the extermination of the royally patronized priests of the alien god—to realize the magnitude of the reaction he now experienced.

Add to this the intensity of his prolonged praying, the long run to Jezreel, and his abstinence from food. He was both physically and emotionally exhausted. He discovered that the laws of nature function entirely without respect of persons and regardless of the merits of the cause that sparks the exhaustion.

Elijah was utterly alone in the desert, for he had left his servant a day's journey away—alone with himself, wallowing in an orgy of self-pity. One would have thought that after the excitement and exhaustion of the previous day he would have reveled in the hours of solitude. But no! Instead, he turned inwards and became vocally sorry for himself. "I have had enough, Lord," he moaned, "take my life."

There was also a psychological cause for his condition. In his hour of extreme reaction he actually reproached God for not adequately rewarding him for the zeal he had displayed in His cause.

"I have been very zealous for the Lord God Almighty," he boasted. In strange disillusionment he said, "I am no better than my ancestors"—tacit admission that he had been cherishing a secret sense of spiritual superiority. (Later the falsity of his assertion was laid bare, for there were seven thousand Israelites who had not bowed the knee to Baal.) His self-esteem was dealt a shattering blow. It seemed that all his zealous service had gone for nothing, unrecognized. He felt utterly let down—alone and lonely. "I only am left."

Elijah's sense of prophetic calling, which till then had been so strong, had now evaporated and he deserted his nation in her hour of need. Had he not prayed and toiled for a mighty spiritual revival to sweep over the land? But to all appearances, the stirring had been superficial and ephemeral. He was an utter failure. Death would be preferable to life.

A COMPASSIONATE GOD
But his God is gracious and compassionate. He did not take His overwrought servant at his word, nor did He even reproach him. ("He knows how we are formed, he remembers that we are dust" [Ps. 103:14].) Instead he dispatched an angelic messenger with a meal cooked in heaven's kitchen. The angel awakened Elijah and bade him eat. After he had satisfied his hunger, a kind sleep overcame him. The operation was repeated a second time.

Strengthened and refreshed by food and rest, Elijah traveled forty days and nights, "until he reached Horeb, the mount of God." Then he went into a cave and spent the night. Only then did God confront him with his fundamental problem. But for him there was no message in the tornado that shattered the rocks, or in the earthquake, or in the accompanying fire. It was not until "after the fire

came a gentle whisper," that God's message pene-
trated his lonely heart (1 Kin. 19:12).

Any who may find themselves nearing the same
condition should note and take comfort from the
divine method used with the overwrought prophet.
In modern theological jargon, Elijah was an ideal
example of "burnout." He displayed all the authentic
marks of that distressing condition.

What was the divine panacea? Two nourishing
meals and two long sleeps. Only then, in a time of
solitude, when he was in a fit state to hear God's
"voice of gentle stillness," was he able to face his
basic spiritual problem. Renewal of his depleted
physical and nervous resources paved the way to a
return to spiritual renewal and usefulness.

The lesson is obvious. It was only when Elijah
was prepared to renounce his self-pity that God's gentle voice became audible to him. God does not shout
His messages. Only then did the dove of peace return
to his heart. Loneliness fled in the face of his renewed
consciousness of the presence of God with him.

To his astonishment, God told him that far from
being alone in his zeal and loyalty to Him, as he had
supposed in his self-pitying mood, there were seven
thousand others who also had refused to bow the
knee to Baal.

Then the Lord assured him that he had not been
laid aside because of his temporary defection. For
him there was still a significant ministry to fulfill.

IMPORTANT SPIRITUAL LESSONS
Several important spiritual lessons emerge that have
a direct bearing upon the evil of self-pity with its con-

sequent sense of loneliness. These lessons should be
mastered by those who are lonely or depressed.

- The Christian cannot with impunity break
  the laws of health, even though it be in an
  endeavor to meet the pressing needs of God's
  service and man's need. The fact that we are
  Christians does not render us immune from
  the penalty of broken natural law.
- Times of solitude in which we withdraw from
  the rush and bustle of daily life are necessary
  wherever possible. It is then we may experience physical and spiritual renewal. It is our
  peril that we overspend our physical and nervous capital.
- If we shift our center from Christ to self, we
  lay ourselves open to attack from our adver-
  sary and expose ourselves to other spiritual
  maladies.
- What in our darker moments we see as failure, may sometimes be more apparent than
  real. In any case, no failure need be final. The
  road to cleansing and forgiveness is always
  open (1 John 1:9).

It was when Elijah threw off his self-pity and
once again turned his eyes toward his compassionate God that deliverance came. A renewed sense of
the divine presence banished his unwarranted sense
of loneliness.

THE PERIL OF SELF-CENTEREDNESS

Another subtle manifestation of the self-life—life

that revolves around oneself—is self-centeredness: becoming almost totally absorbed in one's own interests and concerns. It is a well-known fact that people who are perennially lonely tend to move in this direction, only to find that their loneliness increases in proportion to their self-absorption.

Self is the only prison that can ever bind the soul.
Christ is the only Angel that can the gates unroll.
And when He comes to set thee free,
Arise and follow fast!
His way may lie through darkness,
But it leads to life at last.

Referring to the benefits of wholesome and positive introspection in his book, *The Radiant Life*, W. E. Sangster wrote:

The first thing that strikes any man or woman who seriously conducts this kind of self-examination, is how preoccupied we are with ourselves—not only, or chiefly, when we are engaged in self-examination, but at all times. In the natural man, everything seems to have an immediate self-reference. The instant reaction of normal nature to any event or piece of news, or future possibility is, "How will this affect me?" The average man is far more distressed by a trifling mishap to himself, than by a major calamity in someone else's life. Self-preoccupation is so natural and common that it is accepted as normal; it is only when we make ourselves face it that the enormity and distortion of our selfishness really appears.

It has been plausibly argued that without the aid of self-centeredness, loneliness would find it difficult to exist. If we persist in focusing our thoughts upon ourselves, especially at a time when someone dear to us has been taken from our side, such an attitude will only fuel the fires of our desolation.

If the scriptural model is followed, the Christian life cannot be consistently selfish and self-centered. Christianity is uniformly presented as outward going, caring, concerned. To be Christlike, we will care so much for others that we largely forget ourselves.

Doctors tell of an uncommon nervous disease known as chorea that causes the patient to turn round and continue to spin slowly on one spot—a condition strikingly similar to the conduct of the self-centered person. But all that self-absorption achieves is to imprison the soul in its own misery. Wholesome, constructive introspection can serve a useful purpose, but morbid self-scrutiny is counterproductive.

In *The Way of the Cross,* J. Gregory Mante tells how in the Palace of Wurtzung there is a room where the walls are covered by mirrors. It is called the Hall of a Thousand Mirrors. You enter. A thousand hands are stretched out to meet you, a thousand smiles greet your smile, a thousand pairs of eyes will weep when you weep. But they are all your hands, your smile, your tears. What a picture of the self-centered person! Self all around, self-multiplied.

There is a man who often stands
Between me and Thy glory.
His name is Self, my carnal Self
Stands 'twixt me and Thy glory.
O, mortify him, mortify him,
Put him down my Savior!
Exalt Thyself alone!
Lift high the standard of the Cross
And 'neath its folds
Conceal the standard-bearer.

If instead of turning our eyes inward in self-contemplation we turn them outwards to other lonely hearts, setting ourselves to relieve their distress, we will find that in the process we are breaking out of the constricting shell of our own loneliness.

A friend with whom I was traveling in Asia was killed in a plane crash on his way home. His widow, who was in very delicate health, at first was shattered by the unexpected tragedy. However, when time had in some measure alleviated the acuteness of her loneliness, she began to turn her thoughts away from her own sorrow to that of others in like case. "How could my tragic experience be used by God to help other widows?" she asked herself.

As she prayed, the thought came to her, "You are only one of thousands of widows who are grieving as you are. When you hear of someone who has been widowed, why not write to them and share your own experience of the comfort the Lord can give in the hour of need?"

She acted on this divinely inspired suggestion, and before long a whole new area of ministry opened up to her. When she read in the newspaper of someone who had been widowed, perhaps in an accident, perhaps in similar circumstances, she struck up a correspondence. Many were influenced to turn to God in their sorrow and desolation as a result of her concern. She found that as an unexpected side effect, her own loneliness was largely dissipated.

She could very easily have been self-absorbed in her own grief, loneliness, and ill-health. Instead she found the exquisite joy of mediating the comfort of God.

In an article that appeared in *Crusade* magazine, Mary Endersbee quotes C. S. Lewis, who, out of his own experience, depicts in graphic, almost terrible terms, the danger in becoming self-centered:

> If you want to keep it intact, you must give your heart to no one, not even an animal. Wrap it around carefully with hobbies and little luxuries; avoid all entanglements; lock it up in the casket or coffin of your selfishness. But in that casket, safe, dark, motionless, airless—it will change. It will not be broken, it will become unbreakable, impenetrable, unredeemable. The alternative to tragedy, or at least the risk of tragedy, is damnation. The only place outside of heaven where you can be perfectly safe from all the changes and perturbations of love is hell.

One common characteristic of victims of loneliness is a tendency to blame others for their suffering. But the cause is much more likely to lie at their own door—in their own attitudes, whether conscious or unconscious.

Self-centeredness is natural in a child, but in an adult it is childish, a patent mark of immaturity. Our potential for loneliness is greatly increased when we are preoccupied with ourselves, or when we are unduly critical and intolerant of others. In that state of mind and heart we exude an atmosphere that discourages others from desiring to enter into a close relationship with us.

Charles Durham gives a shrewd analysis of the self-centered life in his book, *When You're Feeling Lonely*:

> The six undesirable personality traits listed here, each have roots somewhere in self-centeredness. The reformers were often power-hungry, the excessive talker needs to be at the center stage, the competitor must be the best, and the angry person must have a vendetta. Boasting is often the expression of excessive pride, or a cover for personal insecurity.

To remedy this unhappy situation, we should undertake a ruthlessly honest reevaluation of our attitudes, painful though the process may prove to be. It will be well worth the pain. Then, having faced reality, heed Paul's injunction and "count yourselves dead to sin [and self] but alive to God" (Rom. 6:11).

14

MINISTERING TO THE LONELY

Alone, alone, all all alone
Alone on a wide, wide sea;
And never a saint took pity on
My soul in agony.
—Samuel Taylor Coleridge

Ministering to the lonely people who surround us is
never an easy task, even when we have the highest
motivation and the utmost goodwill. Friendly
advances are not always easy to make to a person in
the grip of loneliness, nor are they always well
received. Sometimes one will meet with a rebuff. A
positive response on a first approach is unusual.
Even though the sufferer may be aching for friendship, paradoxically for one reason or another he or
she is loath to respond. It is for those who are concerned, and who do not labor under such a handicap,
to be on the lookout for such persons, make the first
approach, and be prepared to accept an initial
rebuff. In this way we can often break through the
ice and open the way for further contact.

On one occasion when my wife and I had gone

to the mountains for a time of retreat, she was brought to face anew the believer's responsibility for personal witness. Being of a shy and retiring disposition, she found witnessing to others a rather daunting experience. However, after meeting with the Lord at this time, she promised Him that henceforth she would be willing to witness for Him to anyone, anytime, anywhere. For her this was a costly commitment.

Only a day or two after our return to the city, as she was walking past an open-air evangelistic service, she noticed a young woman standing alone, listening to the message. As she passed her she felt the prompting of the Holy Spirit to go back and witness to her. Her recent resolve came to mind, so she retraced her steps.

After approaching the young woman, she discovered that she had only that day come to the city from the country, looking for employment. She knew no one and was desperately lonely. After further conversation she committed her life to the Lord, and later became a sincere Christian worker.

We who are enjoying the companionship of Christ should be sensitively alert to such opportunities, for we are surrounded by similarly lonely people who might be led to the Lord through a friendly touch, and find in Him the solution to their problem.

Lonely people often assume a protective mask to conceal their distress. We should be alert to pierce the mask and endeavor to overleap the barrier it creates.

In his *Macbeth,* Shakespeare very graphically poses a question that is relevant for the Christian worker:

Canst thou not minister to a mind diseas'd,
Pluck from the memory a rooted sorrow,
Raze out the hidden troubles of the brain,
And with some sweet oblivious antidote
Cleanse the stuff'd bosom of that perilous stuff
Which weighs upon the heart?

In ministering to the lonely, one productive avenue is that of friendly hospitality. Shyness and reticence can more easily be overcome at the meal table than anywhere else. Attractive food and a friendly exchange of conversation will help to loosen the tongue and create an atmosphere in which it will be easier for the sufferer to unbutton and unburden himself or herself.

Those who have themselves trodden the same lonely path will be especially alive to the situation, and from the background of their own painful experience will be best equipped to help the fellow sufferer out of his or her distress. The fact that we ourselves have known the comfort of God in our lonesomeness lays on us the responsibility of mediating that comfort to others as Paul suggests in 2 Corinthians 1:3–4:

Praise be to the God and Father of our Lord Jesus Christ, the Father of compassion and the God of all comfort, *who comforts us in all our troubles, so that we can comfort those in any trouble* with the comfort we ourselves have received from God (*italics mine*).

Kathleen Parsa, in *Discipleship* magazine,

recounts how simple assurance that God really loved her brought to a woman relief from loneliness.

While traveling recently, I encountered a lonely woman in her mid-twenties in a public restroom. She was depressed and crying because she was far from her homeland of Ireland. She had also been drinking but seemed alert. After blurting out her story, she apologized.

"I am sorry about this," she said.

"Really, it's all right," I assured her. "I've been homesick before myself."

"I had a couple of drinks, but instead of feeling happy, I feel so miserably alone," she confessed.

"Are you a Christian?" I asked, feeling somehow that she might be.

"Yes," she replied.

"Then you know Jesus loves you?" I said.

She paused, looking me straight in the eye. "Yes," she said slowly, "He does."

"Well, even though you feel alone, you are not alone, ever. He's always with you and He'll always love you." I gave her a quick hug and said, "I'll be praying for you."

With that I hurried out, but not without first noticing a change in her countenance. She was smiling, and seemed calmer.

For those who desire to help the lonely, opportunities abound. Visitation in homes for the elderly is appreciated by those who seldom have a visitor. Many old people who live alone in their own homes would eagerly welcome a visitor and a friendly chat.

For those who are in frail health, an offer to cut the lawn or to do other odd jobs that they are unable to do for themselves would be a godsend. In such an atmosphere of goodwill it is not difficult to bring a message of comfort or salvation from the Scriptures.

But it must be borne in mind that ministry to the lonely can be a costly, time-consuming and at times disappointing experience. We cannot genuinely help others without "virtue" going out of us— physical and emotional force. To be effective in this area of service will require us to identify with our friends and to enter into their experience as though it were our own.

PART 2:
PRESCRIBING THE CURE

15

ON THE ROAD TO RELIEF

The Lord, the Lord, the compassionate and gracious
God, slow to anger, abounding in love and faithfulness, maintaining love to thousands, and forgiving
wickedness, rebellion and sin."
—Exodus 34:6–7

It is much easier to diagnose the nature of physical
malady than to prescribe the appropriate remedy—
and it is no different with maladies of the spirit, of
which loneliness is one. The spiritual and physical
afflictions are so diverse in origin, so varied in incidence, and so different in manifestation.

In the doctor-patient relationship, the most sat-
isfactory results are secured when there is complete
openness and sincerity on the part of both doctor
and patient. So must it be if the cause of the loneliness is to be correctly diagnosed and the longed for
remedy prescribed and acted on. As with medicine,
the most helpful prescription is often the most
unpleasant to take. It is only the immature person,
however, who refuses to swallow the curative
medicine because it tastes unpleasant!

Without hesitation I would lay it down as
axiomatic that if loneliness is to be overcome, it

must be accepted that the initiative in relieving the condition lies with those who are suffering. It is they who must take the first step and set the machinery for recovery in motion. If they are unwilling to do this, they are likely to be left with their loneliness.

Ultimately, every one of us must face reality and take responsibility for our condition. It is our personal loneliness, and for it we have final responsibility. So if any change is to be effected, it is we who must take the initiative. If we choose to deny responsibility and blame others for it, the prospect for release is dim. We must cease blaming parents, environment, or other people or circumstances, or there can be no effective strategy for conquering the malady. There is good hope for release when we accept that, in the end, we and no one else are responsible to create the conditions for change.

CLEARING THE GROUND
Loneliness is by no means always spiritual in origin, but spiritual factors may very well accentuate the problem. Since this is very likely to be the case, the ground of our lives should be cleared of all noxious elements so that the Holy Spirit can work unhindered in the soil of our hearts. If there are things we know to be wrong, or about which the Holy Spirit has been convicting us, these should be honestly confessed with no excuses or secret reservations. One evidence that our confession is sincere will be that our sins are not only confessed, but renounced.

Repentance is to leave the sins
We loved before,
And show that we in earnest grieve,
By doing them no more.

If a secret resentment against the Lord is cherished in the heart—and this is often the case, though not openly expressed—this attitude must be corrected. God purposes only good for His child. "God disciplines us *for our good*, that we may share in his holiness" (Heb. 12:10; *italics mine*). We must be right with God before we can be right with ourselves and others.

This process may be likened to the lancing of an infected sore. Before the healing process can begin, the offensive material must be drained off.

When we come to Him in true penitence, God is very gracious. We need entertain no fear of rebuff or rejection, no matter how unworthy we feel and are. His attitude to His failing children is beautifully exhibited in the revelation of Himself God gave to Moses when he prayed, "Now show me your glory" (Ex. 33:18).

And he passed in front of Moses, proclaiming, "The Lord, the Lord, the compassionate and gracious God, slow to anger, abounding in love and faithfulness, maintaining love to thousands, and forgiving wickedness, rebellion and sin" (Ex. 34:6–7).

APPROPRIATING FORGIVENESS
A gift does not become ours until we appropriate it.

God freely offers forgiveness for all our sin, and acceptance of that forgiveness is another important milestone on the road to restoration. Lonely people tend to be self-condemnatory. They see in their condition some real or imaginary fault of their own for which they find it hard to forgive themselves.

But if our holy God is willing, for Christ's sake, to forgive us on confession, then surely we can forgive ourselves for the sins He has forgiven. Hear His assuring words: "For I will forgive their wickedness and will remember their sins no more" (Heb. 8:12).

Why should we keep on remembering and tormenting ourselves when God assures us that He has not only forgiven our sins but forgotten them as well? Is it not unbelief that grieves His loving heart?

One writer termed forgiveness "this amazing therapeutic agent." He asserted that to be able to forgive affords such a relief to the soul that it is all the relief many need. So, if there is someone whom we have not forgiven for some injury suffered, that is a stumbling block that must be removed.

So avail yourself of the therapeutic power of God's ready forgiveness. Take Paul's inspired advice and forget "what is behind" (Phil. 3:13). Resolutely slam and lock the door on past sin and failures, and throw away the key! Then strain forward to the better things that lie ahead.

Do not wait passively (and hopelessly) for someone else to do something about your loneliness. Look life in the face and step resolutely forward. Face reality and adjust to it.

Recently, in counseling a young man who had retreated from life as the result of some very painful experiences, I discovered that through discouragement he had dropped out of social life and had become a "loner." I encouraged him to make a new beginning the very next day, to ask God to enable him once again to establish contact with his fellows and begin serving the Lord again.

The very next evening he came to me with a beaming face. He had approached a non-Christian neighbor whom he found responsive to his advances. The neighbor had actually invited him to come and do some Bible study with him! God does not take long to answer the sincere prayer of one who desires to be right with Him.

SELF-DISCLOSURE

Another helpful step in coping with loneliness is to unburden oneself to God uninhibitedly, just as the psalmist often did. Be open and honest with Him. Tell Him exactly how you feel. He is your heavenly Father, whose sympathetic ear is always open to His children's woes.

> For he knows how we are formed, he remembers that we are dust (Ps. 103:14).
> *Pour out your hearts* to him, for God is our refuge (Ps. 62:8; *italics mine*).

Further, if there is some mature Christian whom you feel you can trust, unburden yourself to him or her. A burden shared is often a burden halved. Share your feelings and failures, your struggles and fears—and your joy as well. In other words, "unbutton" yourself, reveal yourself, weaknesses and all. You will be amazed at the sympathetic hearing you will receive, as well as the therapeutic value of such self-disclosure.

IN ACCEPTANCE LIES PEACE

"In acceptance lies peace" has become almost a spiritual cliché, but it enshrines an important spiritual and psychological truth. We cannot change our outward circumstances. These are beyond our control, and we are responsible only for things under our control. But we can, and should, change our inward attitude to them. By present action we can modify the future. Where no alternative seems possible, it is only common sense to come to terms with life. While this is admittedly a difficult lesson to master, it is an essential one.

Two friends of mine had six children, three of whom had below normal both physical and mental abilities. In the early stages of this experience, my friends found it desperately hard to accept that this was God's will for them; they struggled against it and questioned why this should have happened to them. But they found that, far from helping the situation, they were only hurting themselves and spoiling their lives.

Then, like Jacob, they had a transforming encounter with the Lord. Finally, they accepted the fact that God had permitted this trial and that "in all things God works for the good of those who love him, who have been called according to his purpose" (Rom. 8:28).

"Once we had accepted it as God's will for us," the wife told me, "we learned in experience the truth

---

we had known in theory, that in acceptance lies peace, and we were able to triumph in the midst of the trial." But she added this significant word: "Once we had accepted it as the will of God, it couldn't hurt us any more." So they emerged from the trial enriched, not impoverished.

Note that they accepted the will of God while still in the midst of the trying circumstances, difficult though they were. Then they adapted to the adverse circumstances; and those who knew them testified that they adorned the painful situation. Those three words—accept, adapt, adorn—carry their own message.

It can be so with our loneliness; we can accept it as God's will for us, and also accept the responsibility of triumphantly coping with it. If we react rightly, the whole experience can have a positive benefit. In accepting instead of resenting and rebelling, we find ourselves better able to accept ourselves and others. In the final analysis, the determining factor in the battle with loneliness is our attitude toward it.

The lonely person faces only two possible choices, and the choice he or she makes will determine the possibility of relief. He must either rise above the loneliness, or succumb to it and continue to suffer the consequences.

One can run away from life—and many are taking the suicide route—or look the facts in the face and meet them with the courage God will give.

Now we are in a position to consider some possible courses of action—in addition to those that have already been mentioned—that may greatly relieve or even cure our malady.

16

SEDATIVE, NOT SOLUTION

Although gay companions o'er the bowl
Dispel awhile the sense of ill,
Though pleasures fill the maddening soul,
The heart, the heart is empty still.
—Lord Byron

When one is marooned in the arid wastes of loneliness, concerned and well-meaning friends—out of the kindness of their hearts—offer advice and antidotes that they hope will be of help. But while the kindly gesture is appreciated, the suggestions usually do little to alleviate the anguish of the heart. Suggestions like taking a vacation, joining an encounter group, or buying new clothes, coming at a time when the suffering is acute, are as helpful as telling a neurotic person not to worry or a depressed person to cheer up. They seem to bear no relation to the realities of the situation.

Some such activities doubtless may prove helpful in affording temporary distraction and relief, but they are only a sedative, not a solution, for they touch only the surface of the problem. Sooner or later reality must be honestly faced and the root cause searched out and dealt with.

Alfred Lord Tennyson wrote of the pallid consolations that were extended to him in the tragic hour when his dearest friend was snatched away to a premature grave.

> One writes that "other friends remain,"
> That loss is common to the human race;
> And common is the commonplace,
> And vacant chaff well meant for grain.
>
> That loss is common does not make
> My own loss less bitter, rather more;
> Too common! Never morning wore
> To evening, but some heart did break.
> —In Memoriam A. A. H.

The newly-bereaved widow, for example, is often encouraged by her friends to begin a new career and build a new life for herself. The advice is correct and sound and probably will be acted upon, but at a later date. Then it will have meaning for her. But none of these can fill the present aching void.

Travel, with its new scenes and varied interests, does afford some distraction. But the trouble is that wherever we go we take our loneliness with us—we cannot leave it at home. And when we return from our travel or other activity, we will find it awaiting us when we enter the familiar door. Travel is helpful, but it is only a sedative.

In the rupture of a treasured relationship or in the desolation of bereavement, it is inevitable that we feel acutely alone in our sorrow and loss. It is not that our friends have failed us, or do not love us deeply and desire to help, but they have each other, and their own interests claim their attention. They have other things to talk about and share and may have troubles of their own. But we are shut up with our own lonely heart and there seems no end to the dark tunnel in which we find ourselves.

At first, the very prospect of taking life up again seems too painful to contemplate. Someone must keep the memory of the loved one alive. It would seem almost callous to allow life to go back to normal again as though nothing has happened.

OUTWARD EXPRESSION OF GRIEF

In the shallowness of our modern lifestyle, the outward expression of grief tends to be suppressed, especially on the part of men. But that suppression serves only to generate a deeper loneliness. Grief should be freely expressed, by men as well as women.

In my youth there was a much greater open expression of sorrow and sympathy at the loss of a loved one. Relatives went into mourning, sometimes for as long as six months. Women wore black dresses. Men, and boys even, wore black arm-bands. Handkerchiefs and stationery were edged with black. This was done as a sincere and tangible expression of shared grief and respect.

I do not advocate a return to those practices, but they did allow sorrow and grief to have wholesome and overt expression. It indicated to the bereaved person that they and their loved one were not forgotten.

The prevailing tendency, however, is to avoid talking about the one who has died, for fear of embarrassing the bereaved. But the fact is that, in most cases, the grieving person wants to do that more than anything in the world. Talking about them keeps alive the treasured memory in a wholesome, not a morbid manner. To be able to talk about a departed loved one in a natural way is a most valuable therapy.

The lonely heart, as we have seen, seeks escape from its prison house in many ways. Some flee from reality by plunging into a round of frenzied activity, in the vain hope that this will fill the endless hours and perhaps induce a period of forgetfulness. Others resort to excursions into the world of entertainment but find that it provides only fleeting relief.

The murky world of the occult makes its appeal to those who desire to reestablish contact with loved ones beyond the veil. Eastern religions have become very popular and are increasingly making their appeal to a segment of society, disillusioned and lost. But all these prove a delusion and disappointment.

"Everyone has escapes," writes Nancy Potts in her book, *Living Between the Times*. "Some people overeat, others watch TV soap operas, become workaholics, enter on nonstop activities . . . try to dull the pain with alcohol or drugs. The possible ways to escape are endless. However, the end result is self-pity and a loss of self-respect."

This is not to say that some of these escapes do not in measure meet a need, but the relief they give is short-lived. They are not solutions, only sedatives. A band-aid is useful to cover a cut, but is not of much help to a broken arm. Tranquilizers may afford temporary relief, but address only the periphery of the problem. They fail to treat the real focus of infection from which the loneliness stems.

The round of pleasure or the amassing of wealth are but vain attempts to escape from the persistent ache. It is a well-known fact that the millionaire is usually a lonely man, and the comedian is often more unhappy than members of the audience he is entertaining.

Even success does not always fill the aching void, as the brilliant Henry Martyn discovered. At the age of twenty, as a student at Cambridge University, he gained the highest honors the world had to offer in mathematics. But when the celebrations were over, Martyn said that, instead of his success bringing fulfillment, "to my surprise I found that I had only grasped a shadow."

Later he went to India as a missionary. When he reached that land, he knelt on the shore and prayed, "And now let me burn out for God." He lived for only seven more years, but in that short time he gave the world translations of the New Testament in three difficult Eastern languages. Those three New Testaments were no shadow!

NO SIMPLE CURE

We must face the unadorned fact that our loneliness will not be dissipated by any simple or single procedure. It is usually too deeply ingrained into our personality and emotional makeup to respond to anything but radical treatment.

Nor will the final answer be found in forming a

number of casual relationships. It will be discovered in forming quality relationships with congenial persons. It is not the number of friends we gain that is important, but rather the quality of relationship we establish. As Seneca said, "We are born to live together." Life is not complete alone.

In each of us there is a deep psychological need and desire for a warm companionship that will survive the tests of time and modern pressured life. Even our divine Lord, self-sufficient though He was, in His human nature craved the friendship and support of His intimates. Under stress their friendship proved imperfect, but it was something He appreciated deeply. Indeed, He paid a lovely tribute to their loyalty in the memorable words: "You are those who have stood by me in my trials" (Luke 22:28).

Intimacy with sympathetic and understanding friends can and does alleviate the pangs of loneliness. And although it may prove difficult to achieve that intimacy, it is possible if approached in the right manner and with purpose of heart.

17

THE BALM OF FRIENDSHIP

Friendship is a thing most necessary to life—since
without friends, no one would choose to live, though
possessed of all other advantages.
—Aristotle

A warm, stable friendship is one of the most precious gifts life has to offer. Its absence is one of life's
greatest deprivations. Apart from the mutual joy
that we derive from the relationship, friends are one
of the most effective barriers against loneliness.

In his useful book, *Friends and Friendship,*
Jerry White defines friendship in these terms: "A
friend is a trusted confident to whom I am mutually
drawn as a companion and ally, whose love for me is
not dependent on my performance, and whose influence draws me nearer to the Lord."

In a true friendship there is a mutual willingness for each to accept the other just as they are,
warts and all. Those who establish such a relationship are rich indeed.

George Elliott describes such a friendship: "O
the inexpressible comfort of feeling safe with someone, having to weigh neither thoughts nor measure
words, but pour them all out just as they are, chaff

and grain together; and a faithful hand will take and sift them, keep what is worth keeping, and with a breath of kindness, blow the rest away."

When Jeremy Taylor, the old Puritan, had his house burgled, all his choicest possessions taken, and his family turned out of doors, he knelt down and thanked God that his enemies had left him the sun and moon, a loving wife and many friends to pity and relieve, the providence of God, all the promises of the gospel, his faith, his hope of heaven, and his charity towards his enemies!

With wealth such as this, no burglar could impoverish him, for true riches do not consist merely in material things. "Many friends to pity and relieve."

THE RISK OF FRIENDSHIP

It is the "how" of establishing a friendship that creates the problem for the lonely person. Either by choice or by exclusion they find themselves isolated from their fellows. As we have seen, either by shyness or the fear of possible rebuff, they have been held back from attempting friendly approaches.

They feel it almost impossible to take the first step towards closer contact with others. And yet, if there is to be any relief from loneliness, those advances must be made, and made by them. Otherwise they will continue to be confined in their self-constructed prison house. It is a well-proved principle that "a man that hath friends must show himself friendly" (Prov. 18:24 KJV).

There are hermit souls that live withdrawn
in the peace of their self-content.

There are souls that dwell like stars apart
    in a fellow-less firmament.
There are pioneer souls who blaze their paths
    where highways never ran,
But let me live in a house by the side of the road
    and be a friend of man.

There are ways, however, by which even the shy and withdrawn person can overleap this barrier, but it will take a deliberate act of the will to locate and establish and maintain the friendship. We tend to believe that friendship depends on meeting the right people. God in His Word tells us it depends on our being the right person.

In *The Friendly Male*, D. W. Smith tells how one researcher circulated a questionnaire probing the nature of friendship. In every answer he received, the respondent said that those closest to them were people willing to disclose their feelings and needs. "We often fail to open ourselves to others from fear of rejection," Smith concludes. "If you open up, you take a risk, you become vulnerable."

That is undoubtedly true. But is the alternative if we do not take the risk more acceptable? It means an unending perpetuation of the painful status quo.

Ralph Waldo Emerson asked a pertinent question: "We take care of our health, we lay up money, we keep our roof tight and our clothing sufficient, but who provides wisely that he shall not be wanting in the best property of all—friends?"

True friendship can be costly. It is much more than making use of someone for our own benefit, for of necessity it involves self-giving, and that incurs a cost. It was said of a wealthy and generous man that with all his giving, he never gave himself. He thus withheld the most precious gift of all.

FRIENDSHIP CAN TRANSFORM

On returning home from her first summer camp, a young girl was asked whether she had felt lonely or homesick. Her ingenuous reply was, "I had no time to be lonely. Because I was so busy keeping other girls from being homesick, I never thought of being homesick myself." What a window into the way out of loneliness! It is the self-occupied person who feels its sharpest pangs. Friendliness begets friendship and in the process banishes loneliness.

The establishing of a friendship at a critical junction in the young Hudson Taylor's missionary career played a significant part in the whole of his subsequent missionary achievements. After he had experienced two crushing blows, God brought into his life a godly Scottish minister, William Burns, a man about twenty years his senior. Burns had been the human instrument in a powerful spiritual revival at the church of the saintly Robert Murray McCheyne in Dundee.

For seven months the two friends worked and traveled and prayed together, months that left an indelible impression on the younger man. One of the biographies of Hudson Taylor highlights the importance of that timely friendship. It was rightly said that Burns saved Taylor from himself. Rejected by conventional missionaries as he was, he might have grown into an isolated snob, for he was far ahead of his times. He might have developed into an individualist moving in steadily contracting circles, leaving little behind but a few converts and an awkward memory. Instead, he became a trail-blazer of the modern missionary movement.

He received from Burns an imprint that was never obliterated. His experience exemplified the value of a quality friendship, which came at a time when, in his loneliness, he might have turned in on himself.

THE IMPORTANCE OF LOYALTY

Once a friendship has been established, we should keep in mind that mutual loyalty is essential if it is to flourish and endure. One researcher discovered that the qualities most appreciated in a friendship were: the ability to keep a confidence, loyalty, warmth and affection, and the ability to have intimate conversations. Those in search of friendship should bear these findings in mind, for it is a two-way business.

Confidences should be kept in sacred trust and not shared with others, even for prayer, without the consent of the friend. Many promising friendships have foundered because this factor has not been observed.

Ben Johnson gave this counsel: "A man should always keep his friendship in repair." One way of doing this when separated is through a warm correspondence. This will build an added dimension to the relationship.

A friendship flourishes and deepens in proportion to what each party puts into it. It must be worked at and mutual unselfishness is a valuable component. Working together in social or Christian service will forge a close bond.

Paul the apostle possessed the ability to gain

and retain the loyalty of his friends of both sexes and all ages, to a remarkable degree. The secret of this gift peeps out in all his letters—his capacity for unselfish and undemanding love. He was prepared to pour it out without stint, even if it met with no return. "I will very gladly spend for you everything I have and expend myself as well. If I love you more, will you love me less?" (2 Cor. 12:15).

F. W. H. Myers captures this quality in his poem, "St. Paul."

> Hearts I have won, of sister or of brother,
> Quick on earth, or buried in the sod,
> Lo, every heart awaiteth me, another
> Friend in the blameless family of God.

But there is a friendship that is even more important and wonderful, which should be cultivated persistently. A friendship which, if truly embraced and responded to, will banish loneliness. The wise man of the Proverbs wrote, "There are friends who pretend to be friends, but *there is a friend who sticks closer than a brother*" (Prov. 18:24 RSV; *italics mine*).

> Many names are dear, but His is dearer
> How it grows more dear as life goes on;
> Many friends are dear, but He is dearer,
> Always what we want, and all our own.
> Jesus, Jesus let us ever say it
> Softly to ourselves as some sweet spell;
> Jesus, Jesus, troubled spirit lay it
> On thy heart, and it will make thee well.
> —A. J. Foxwell

18

PSYCHOLOGICAL AND SOCIAL ELEMENTS

Contrary to what might be expected, I look back on
experiences that at the time seemed especially desolating and painful with particular satisfaction. Indeed, I
can say with complete truthfulness that everything I
have learned in my seventy-five years in this world,
everything that has truly enhanced and enlightened my
existence, has been through affliction and not through
happiness, whether pursued or attained.
                                   —Malcolm Muggeridge

Some writers who approach this subject from the
Christian point of view focus mainly on spiritual
solutions. These are undoubtedly relevant and of
prime importance, but there are psychological and
social factors involved that should not be ignored.
The New Testament blends both approaches.

THE PSYCHOLOGICAL ELEMENT
Before considering what practical steps can be taken
to resolve the problem, one's thinking must be clari-
fied, for it is in the thought life that the battle for
victory must be fought and won.

It must be accepted that some degree of loneliness is a natural component of ordinary living. No one escapes its inroads altogether. The fact that loneliness was an element in the experience of our sinless Lord when He assumed our human nature argues this. We are private beings who do not always admit even our dearest friends into all areas of our private lives.

There are certain walks of life, for example, in which some degree of loneliness is inevitable. Responsible top leadership necessarily involves it, for important and far-reaching decisions have to be made alone—they cannot be shared.

Again, life is so complex that we have to learn to live with some problems of body and mind. God does not remove every adverse circumstance from the path of the Christian or provide easy explanations and solutions to every mysterious dealing. Life would be greatly impoverished were this not so. It is wrestling with adverse circumstances that builds moral and spiritual muscle. If life were all easy and uncomplicated, we would become little better than the spineless jellyfish. While God may allow the thorn to remain, He will also give adequate grace to bear it (2 Cor. 12:9).

In an insightful moment of self-revelation, Malcolm Muggeridge paid striking testimony to the enduring value of the unexplained and painful experiences of life.

> Contrary to what might be expected, I look back on experiences that at the time seemed especially desolating and painful with particular satisfaction. Indeed, I can

say with complete truthfulness that everything I have learned in my seventy-five years in this world, everything that has truly enhanced and enlightened my existence, has been through affliction and not through happiness, whether pursued or attained.

In other words, if it were ever to be possible to eliminate affliction from our earthly existence by means of some drug or medical mumbo-jumbo . . . the result would not be to make life delectable, but to make it too banal and trivial to be endurable.

—*A Twentieth Century Testimony*

It is the tree that has to withstand the fiercest storms that becomes deep-rooted and strong. The fight to overcome or compensate for our loneliness may well prove to be the very agent that drives us to God and makes us strong in ourselves and therefore able to help others in a like condition.

IMPORTANCE OF SELF-DISCLOSURE

If the healing process is to progress, there must be some degree of self-disclosure to someone, a willingness to open and expose oneself. The very articulation of our emotions often sets us on the road to release. If loneliness has caused bitterness, resentment, envy, or self-pity, open your heart first to God and confess these sins, for all sin is primarily against God (Ps. 51:4). Then, if there has been sin against another person, confess it to him or her. We have the healing assurance from God that "if we confess our sins, he is faithful and just and will forgive us our sins and purify us from all unrighteousness" (1 John 1:9).

Confession and acceptance of God's promised forgiveness help to get these negative and harmful attitudes out of our system and will bring unimaginable release. If you can share your emotional problem with another human being, that will also have a most helpful therapeutic effect. Friendship develops and deepens with mutual self-disclosure, for it provides an outlet for the pent-up emotion that produces the loneliness.

It is instructive to note that in the lonely year during which King David was unwilling to open himself and confess his sin with Bathsheba, his attitude locked him into himself. But when he articulated it in a sincere confession, his spirit broke free:

When I kept silent, my bones wasted away through my groaning all day long. For day and night your hand was heavy upon me; my strength was sapped as in the heat of summer. *Then I acknowledged my sin to you and did not cover up my iniquity.* I said, "I will confess my transgressions to the Lord"—*and you forgave the guilt of my sin* (Ps. 32:3–5; *italics mine*).

There is no one, however competent and confident they may appear, who does not have some areas of weakness and some negative attitudes to overcome. We are not unique in that respect. While we cannot change our circumstances, we can change our attitude towards them. Instead of allowing them to shape our lives, we can make them tributary to our growth in maturity. It is only common wisdom to accept what can't be changed and endeavor to change what can be changed.

One reason that might prevent self-disclosure could be a distrust of others. We may feel that if we reveal what we really are like, we will be rejected or betrayed. This is, of course, a possibility. But if we are ever to break free from our bondage, it is a risk that must be be taken. Generally speaking, it will be found that our fear was without foundation. But when the alternative of continuing to live with our unrelieved loneliness is considered, it is a risk well worth taking. Retreating into one's shell achieves nothing.

AVOID SELF-DEPRECIATION
A habit that should be resisted is the tendency to depreciate oneself. This can be at the same time the cause and the result of loneliness. The person who has an unduly low level of self-esteem is especially vulnerable. While we must forsake pride and vanity, Scripture encourages us to make an honest self-appraisal, neither exalting ourselves on the one hand nor depreciating ourselves on the other. Paul emphasizes this in Romans 12:3 when he writes:

> As your spiritual teacher I give this piece of advice to each one of you. Don't cherish exaggerated ideas of your importance, *but try to have a sane estimate of your capabilities* by the light of the faith that God has given to you all (J. B. Phillips).

This does not mean that we are to be satisfied with ourselves as we are—we should be aiming higher, always—but we must not fly to the opposite extreme and devalue ourselves. We should guard against devaluing what God valued so highly as to consider it worth the sacrifice of His Son.

Paul is not speaking here of self-occupation but sane self-evaluation. While he confessed, "I know that nothing good lives in me, that is, in my sinful nature" (Rom. 7:18), that fact did not prevent his honest self-appraisal when he claimed, "I do not think I am in the least inferior to those 'super-apostles' " (2 Cor. 11:5).

God's evaluation of us is more accurate than our own. He knows all about us, for He made us. His estimate of our worth in His sight is measured by the fact that He gave up His Son for us. "God does not show favoritism" (Acts 10:34). Others may seem more attractive and worthy in our eyes, but none is more precious to God than we are.

Paul mastered the secret of handling adverse circumstances.

> *I have learned* to be content whatever the circumstances. I know what it is to be in need, and I know what it is to have plenty. *I have learned the secret* of being content in any and every situation . . . . I can do everything *through him who gives me strength* (Phil. 4:11–13; *italics mine*).

To discover the kind of circumstances he learned to triumph over, read 2 Corinthians 11:23–

28! But note that he emphasizes that it had been a learning process. He had not always been content. He persevered and mastered the secret, through the strength he drew from Christ.

Since self-absorption proves counter-productive in relieving loneliness, the most helpful and sensible alternative is to turn one's thoughts outward to others who may be even more lonely. Think of ways in which you might minister to their need. Think of lonely and neglected children, lonely widows and widowers, lonely divorcees, lonely immigrants or international students. Indeed, your next-door neighbor may be facing the very same problem, without your suspecting it.

In every heart there is the insatiable longing, not always recognized as such, to be loved and appreciated. Form the decision to relate to some such person or persons, and then *do it!*

THE SOCIAL ELEMENT

It is in the area of social relationships that the problem lies. The root of loneliness is the absence of loving and satisfying companionship, and it is here a change must be made.

I take for granted that you are sufficiently earnest to find a remedy for your condition as to be willing to take positive steps towards a solution. Without this sincerity, no suggestion will be of much help. There are only two alternatives—transcend or succumb. The decision to take steps to relate to others is a simple decision of the will, though it may be difficult. But it can lead to a transformed life.

SUGGESTED STEPS

After prayer, think of the most likely person to whom you could make friendly overtures; then seek a favorable opportunity for your contact. Consider the most suitable approach you could make. Practice the art of opening and continuing a conversation.

If there are common interests, begin with those. You will find that one of the most productive methods is to get the other person talking about himself and his interests. This creates a relaxed atmosphere. Being an interested listener paves the way for further communication. Let your interest in him be genuine and you will soon find that you can forget yourself.

Don't be discouraged if the first contact does not develop into a full friendship. The ice has been broken, and that is an important beginning. Don't allow an initial disappointment to deter you from further attempts.

If a friendship does develop, cultivate openness and loyalty from the very first. Broken confidences result in a ruptured friendship. In your own neighborhood, show yourself friendly and loyal so that you will come to be an accepted and trusted part of the community.

It takes two to build a relationship and it does not always blossom overnight. Bear in mind that it is the *quality,* not the *number,* of relationships that is important. Friendship is not automatically maintained, it must be worked at.

There are various activities that can introduce one to rewarding social involvement. Volunteer groups engage in valuable social and philanthropic services—Meals on Wheels, Lifeline, and similar organizations. Additional volunteers are always welcome. Volunteers to help with slow-learning children will meet a warm welcome.

In many larger cities the increase in crime has given birth to neighborhood watch groups. Membership in one of these would lead to a friendly touch with neighbors in a nonthreatening relationship.

Ideally, the church should be the place where loving care and fellowship are extended. Very often this is the case, but unfortunately that ideal is not always realized. A growing number of churches are fully alive to the social implications of the gospel and endeavor to provide services for the suffering and unprivileged. The state, too, is paying more attention to the social needs of its citizens.

Many enduring friendships have been initiated through taking someone out for a meal. Lonely international students respond with almost pathetic eagerness to such an approach. Many never get an invitation into the home of the host country. Over a meal, conversation is relaxed and the suggested gambit of asking the guest about himself or herself, and his or her homeland, will meet with a warm response.

It is when we shift the focus from our own loneliness to relieving that of another sufferer that the healing process gathers momentum in our own lives.

19

THE SPIRITUAL ELEMENT

The Lord has promised good to me,
His word my hope secures,
He will my shield and portion be
As long as life endures.
—John Newton, "Amazing Grace"

"Where is God when I am lonely?" is a question asked by many a depressed person. It may not be actually articulated but it is there deep down nonetheless. Of course the answer is, "Right beside you."

"Whether we feel it or not," writes Margaret Clarkson in *Decision* magazine, "we have His presence for our loneliness, His understanding for the human misunderstanding that ruthlessly assaults our quivering sensitivities, His unchanging and unchangeable purpose for the seeming hopelessness of our frustration and apparent uselessness. . . . Our very infirmities can open up our lives to more of the power of Christ."

Scripture abounds in promises, divine undertakings that await our appropriation. There is no conceivable situation for which there is no appropriate promise. Be alert as you read the Bible to dis-

165

cover what God has promised to do and then lay hold of it. Say to the Lord, "Do as you have said." Promises must be claimed by faith. It was by faith the patriarchs received the promises. Abraham had an abounding confidence in his God. He was "fully persuaded that God had power to do what he had promised" (Rom. 4:21).

Some have difficulty in appropriating for themselves the promises of the Old Testament, which were made, in the main, to Israel. They feel that to lay claim would be like opening a letter addressed to someone else. But Paul answers that problem: "If you belong to Christ, then *you are Abraham's seed, and heirs* according to the promise" (Gal. 3:29; *italics mine*).

The validity of a promise depends upon the character and resources of the one who makes it. God's holy character and boundless resources make His promises credible.

"Every promise is a writing of God," said Charles Spurgeon, "which may be pleaded before Him with the reasonable request, 'Do as Thou hast said.' The Creator will not cheat the creature who depends upon His truth, and far more, the heavenly Father will not break His word to His own child."

God's promises are bound up with His character and rest on four of His attributes.
- His *truth,* which renders lying impossible.
- His *omniscience,* which makes His being deceived or mistaken impossible.
- His *immutability,* which renders change or vacillation impossible.
- His *omnipotence,* which makes anything possible.

So, when we come to God armed with one of His promises, we can do so with the utmost confidence, for "He who promised is faithful." If there seems to be a yawning gap between God's promises and our experience of their fulfillment, it is because we have not bestirred ourselves to claim them.

John Bunyan quaintly described his experience in endeavoring to appropriate one of the promises: "Satan would labor to pull the promise away from me, telling me that Christ did not mean *me* in John 6:37. He pulled and I pulled. But, God be praised, I got the better of him." Bunyan has not been alone in this representative experience.

THREE POSSIBLE ATTITUDES

We can adopt one of three attitudes in relation to God's promises:

1. We can *"come short"* of them by devaluing them to the level of our past experience (Rom. 3:23 KJV). It is possible for us so to tone them down that we come far short of what God is offering.

2. We can *"stagger"* or *"waver"* because of our unbelief, either because of the risk involved or because the promise seems too good to be true (Rom. 4:20). But the one who wavers misses the blessing, "That man should not think he will receive anything from the Lord" (James 1:7).

3. We can be *"fully assured"* of God's trustworthiness and receive the promises. Abraham the father of the faithful, was "fully persuaded that God had power to do what he

167

had promised" (Rom. 4:21), and therefore he "did not waver through unbelief" (v. 20).

With God, promise and performance are inseparable. So take some of the great promises of Scripture and, with them under your feet, step out in confidence. Here are some of God's undertakings that have special relevance to the problem of loneliness.

Do not fear, *for I am with you;* do not be dismayed, for I am your God. I will strengthen you and help you; I will uphold you with my righteous right hand (Is. 41:10; *italics mine*).

My presence will go with you, and I will give you rest (Ex. 33:14; *italics mine*).

When you pass through the waters, *I will be with you;* and when you pass through the rivers, they will not sweep over you. When you walk through the fire, you will not be burned; the flames will not set you ablaze. For I am the Lord, your God . . . . Do not be afraid, for *I am with you* (Is. 43:2–3, 5; *italics mine*).

Adopt Paul's attitude toward these divine undertakings: "I have faith in God that it will happen just as he told me" (Acts 27:25).

POSITIVE STEPS TO RELIEF

Whatever is true, whatever is noble, whatever is right, whatever is pure, whatever is lovely, whatever is admirable—if anything is excellent or praiseworthy—think about such things.

—Philippians 4:8

Once the initial mental decision to take the initiative in establishing new relationships has been taken, positive practical steps must follow to support and implement that decision. It is so easy to yield to inertia where motivation is weak. And it is you who must supply the motivation. Already a number of possible steps have been suggested, but others follow.

PURSUE A SUITABLE DIVERSION
The person who has a hobby to fall back upon is fortunate indeed. Some counselors go so far as to assert that no one is really happy or safe without a hobby, and that it makes little difference what outside interest it is a person takes up.

That statement is probably too sweeping, but there is much truth in it. Those who have cultivated no interest outside their normal work are among the most unhappy people when they retire. Without the interest of their accustomed vocation they become bored, lonely, and very sorry for themselves. But it is never too late to take up some congenial hobby.

I personally have found gardening the most absorbing, refreshing, and even exciting of hobbies. Few occupations can fill the lonely hours so rewardingly. To create beauty that gives both pleasure and profit to oneself and others is one of the most enjoyable and fruitful avocations.

One of the benefits of gardening as a hobby is that it has some form that is adapted to people of every age and in every stage of health. It can be engaged in outside or inside and at any time. Even invalids can derive great enjoyment from indoor gardening.

For those blessed with good health, there are many outdoor games available to both men and women, at any stage of life. Apart from the enjoyment of the game itself, participation brings one into close and friendly contact with others in a relaxed atmosphere.

Another most helpful therapy, and one that can be engaged in alone, is walking. It stimulates the respiratory system, purifies the blood, makes one feel more alive and better able to cope with life's demands. Further, it gets one out of the house and into God's wonderful world of nature. In countries where winters are severe, many older people have even found walking under cover in a large shopping mall a healthy and mind-refreshing exercise.

For those who are musically inclined, there is an abundance of music to suit every taste, either on one's own stereo or on the radio. In North America especially, there are stations that specialize in Christian music on several levels. Good music is uplifting and meets our aesthetic needs.

For some who are suitably qualified, joining a choir, orchestra, or singing group would, in itself, be a fulfilling experience. In addition, it is an excellent means of establishing contact with people of similar tastes.

Some with a scholastic bent have found release and fulfillment in enrolling for a degree or other course of study that had not been possible to take earlier in life. Many women are adopting this avenue when their children leave home.

In the wide field of art, many options are open to those willing to make the venture. My wife discovered late in life that she had an unusual gift in painting that had lain unused for most of her life. Many of us have undiscovered talents waiting for release. In addition to painting, other options are pottery, china painting, weaving, woodwork, all forms of fancy work, and many others.

Where one has the requisite skill and teaching ability, a class in some practical subject could be commenced for younger people who are unemployed, or who might otherwise be roaming the streets. A friend has turned his large garage into a woodwork shop where he instructs young men in woodturning and kindred work. In the process he is able to influence them for Christ.

In cities where there is an ethnic mix, there are many opportunities for helpful ministry to immigrants or overseas students. Two friends of mine

171

used their home and their spare time to teach them English. As a result of their friendship and interest, a Korean and a Chinese church each had its birth in this home and are now functioning independently.

It is possible to have fellowship with the great minds of all ages and in every sphere through reading good literature. The range of literature available in our libraries is almost unlimited. Books serious and humorous, light and heavy, educative and diverting, religious and secular, are available at little cost.

Even if one has not had much time or taste for reading in the past, there will never be a more appropriate time to cultivate the habit than now. When physical powers wane, one can still read. Begin with books that grip and hold the interest. Then, when the reading habit has been formed, graduate to heavier and more serious subjects. It has been found that housewives who make a practice of reading are less lonely than their peers who are pursuing careers.

Where living conditions are favorable, many lonely people have found great comfort in keeping a pet, having something to love and receiving some measure of affection in return. The obvious welcome of a pet on one's return to an empty house or apartment helps to banish loneliness.

THINK POSITIVELY

We choose what our mind feeds upon, and what we read unconsciously molds our patterns of thought. If we surfeit our minds with negative thoughts, the result is predictable. We can program our mental computer with thoughts that induce loneliness or with thoughts that will banish it. This lies within our choice.

When visiting Hong Kong, a preacher was intrigued by a shop in which tattooing was done. In the window he noticed a number of mottos that were suggested for choice. Among them was "Born to fail."

"But surely no one would choose that motto, would they?" he asked the Chinese tattooist.

"Yes they do," was the reply.

"But why would they choose that one?"

The discerning reply was: "Before they tattoo on chest, they tattoo on mind."

Unconsciously he was giving his version of the Bible statement, "As he thinketh in his heart, so is he" (Prov. 23:7 KJV).

Paul gives a prescription for the kind of thoughts that we should feed into our minds:

> Whatever is true, whatever is noble, whatever is right, whatever is pure, whatever is lovely, whatever is admirable—if anything is excellent or praiseworthy—*think about such things* (Phil. 4:8; *italics mine*).

Since we are commanded to think of these things, it follows that it is in our power to control our thoughts and concentrate them on positive and pleasurable concepts. They automatically exclude the opposite.

We choose the thoughts on which we will meditate, for it is our wills that control mental processes.

A will firmly engaged with God can swing the intellectual processes around to think on holy things.

The best thoughts to entertain are the thoughts of God. Thus, regular reading and meditating on scriptural truth is one of the best ways to exclude thoughts that create or feed loneliness.

Note to the Reader

The publisher invites you to share your response to the message of this book by writing Discovery House Publishers, P.O. Box 3566, Grand Rapids, MI 49501 U.S.A. or by calling 800-283-8333. For information about other Discovery House publications, contact us at the same address and phone number.

SCRIPTURE SUMMARIES ON LONELINESS

God's Original Provision for Loneliness
Genesis 1:27–31; 2:18–22

Causes of Loneliness
Psalm 32:3–5; Habakkuk 1:2–3; Matthew 28:17; Mark 4:15

Examples of Loneliness
Jacob: Genesis 32:24
Elijah: 1 Kings 19:3–4, 10, 12
Enoch: Jude 14–15
Jonah: Jonah 2:2–6

The Loneliness of Leadership
Moses: Exodus 18:17–23; Numbers 11:14; 12:1–2
John the Baptist: Matthew 11:7–11; Luke 1:80
Paul: 2 Corinthians 1:8–9; 11:23–28; 2 Timothy 1:15

The Loneliness of Widowhood
Exodus 22:22–23; Deuteronomy 24:17 19; Psalm 68:5, Acts 6:1–3; 1 Timothy 5:3–16; James 1:27

Principles of Relief from Loneliness and Its Symptoms
Exodus 33:13; 34:6–7; Psalm 25:1, 16, 21; 32:1–6; 51:4; 62:8; 71:17–18; 73:2–5, 16–17; 103:14; Proverbs 18:24; Ecclesiastes 4:9–11; Isaiah 41:10; 61:1–3; Matthew 6:12; 19:12; Luke 22:28; John 13:7; 16:32; Acts 20:35; 21:8–9; 27:25; Romans 7:18; 8:28; 12:3; 1 Corinthians 7:1, 7–8, 25–26; 2 Corinthians 1:3–4; 11:5; 12:9, 15; Galatians 3:29; Philippians 3:13; 4:8, 11–13; Hebrews 8:12; 12:10–12

Attitudes Toward God's Promises Regarding Loneliness
Exodus 33:14; Romans 3:25; 4:20, 21; James 1:6–7

STEPS TO PEACE WITH GOD

1. RECOGNIZE GOD'S PLAN—PEACE AND LIFE

The message you have read in this book stresses that God loves you and wants you to experience His peace and life.

The BIBLE says . . . *"For God loved the world so much that He gave His only Son, so that everyone who believes in Him may not die but have eternal life." John 3:16*

2. REALIZE OUR PROBLEM—SEPARATION

People choose to disobey God and go their own way. This results in separation from God.

The BIBLE says . . . *"Everyone has sinned and is far away from God's saving presence." Romans 3:23*

3. RESPOND TO GOD'S REMEDY—CROSS OF CHRIST

God sent His Son to bridge the gap. Christ did this by paying the penalty of our sins when He died on the cross and rose from the grave.

The BIBLE says . . . *"But God has shown us how much He loves us—it was while we were still sinners that Christ died for us!" Romans 5:8*

4. RECEIVE GOD'S SON—LORD AND SAVIOR

You cross the bridge into God's family when you ask Christ to come into your life.

The BIBLE says . . . *"Some, however, did receive Him and believed in Him; so He gave them the right to become God's children." John 1:12*

THE INVITATION IS TO:

REPENT (turn from your sins) and by faith RECEIVE Jesus Christ into your heart and life and follow Him in obedience as your Lord and Savior.

PRAYER OF COMMITMENT

"Lord Jesus, I know I am a sinner. I believe You died for my sins. Right now, I turn from my sins and open the door of my heart and life. I receive You as my personal Lord and Savior. Thank You for saving me now. Amen."

If you want further help in the decision you have made, write to:
Billy Graham Evangelistic Association, P.O. Box 779, Minneapolis, MN 55440-0779